CW00506216

THE FEW
WHO FLEW

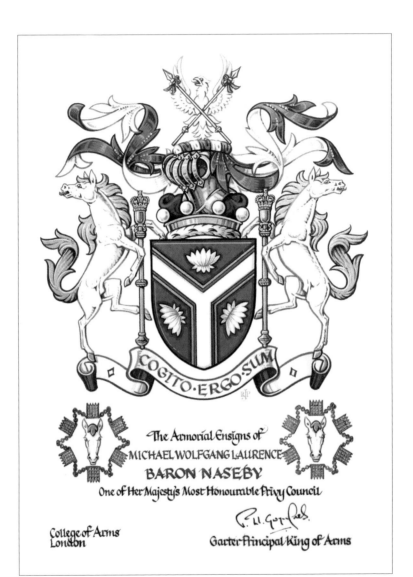

COGITO · ERGO · SUM

The Armorial Ensigns of
MICHAEL WOLFGANG LAURENCE
BARON NASEBY
One of Her Majesty's Most Honourable Privy Council

College of Arms
London

Garter Principal King of Arms

To Shaakirah, Raheema & Aleeyah.
Wonderful names from a wonderful
country.

THE FEW
WHO
FLEW

**RAF National Service
Pilots 1955–1957**

Naseby May 2022

MICHAEL NASEBY
The Rt Hon. The Lord Naseby PC

UNICORN

Published in the UK by Unicorn
an imprint of Unicorn Publishing Group, 2022
Charleston Studio
Meadow Business Centre
Lewes BN8 5RW

www.unicornpublishing.org

All rights reserved. No part of this publication may be reproduced,
stored in or introduced into a retrieval system, or transmitted, in
any form or by any means (electronic, mechanical, photocopying,
recording or otherwise), without the prior written permission of the
copyright holder and the above publisher of this book.

Every effort has been made to trace copyright holders and to obtain
their permission for the use of copyrighted material. The publisher
apologises for any errors or omissions and would be grateful to be
notified of any corrections that should be incorporated in future reprints
or editions of this book.

All photos are from the author's own collection unless otherwise
credited.

© Michael Naseby, 2022

10 9 8 7 6 5 4 3 2 1

ISBN 978-1-914414-48-0

Typesetting by Vivian Head

Printed by Short Run Press, Exeter

DEDICATION

This book is dedicated to my seven grandchildren: Oliver, Ciara, Ella, Jan, Maya, Izzy and Emma.

It is my hope that the experiences recorded in this book and the important lessons that I learned during my time as a National Service pilot will inspire similar values in those who read it: thinking before acting, being independent and adventurous. Above all, may the thrill and my love of flying inspire them to enjoy all the opportunities this wonderful world has to offer.

£2 from the sale of this book will be given to the Royal Air Forces Association

(Registered Charity No. 226686 England & Wales)

ROYAL AIR FORCES Association
The charity that supports the RAF family

CONTENTS

FOREWORD BY THE LORD STIRRUP 7

FOREWORD BY THE VISCOUNT TRENCHARD . . . 8

INTRODUCTION 9

CHAPTER ONE   ANOTHER BIGGLES 11

CHAPTER TWO   AVIATION IN ITS INFANCY 23

CHAPTER THREE   THE PARLIAMENTARY GENESIS OF THE
NATIONAL SERVICE BILL 27

CHAPTER FOUR   CATFORD TO CANADA 37

CHAPTER FIVE   BOUND FOR CANADA 47

CHAPTER SIX   RCAF MOOSE JAW – EARLY DAYS 57

CHAPTER SEVEN   SUMMER LEAVE 69

CHAPTER EIGHT   REAL FLYING TOWARDS WINGS 83

CHAPTER NINE   RCAF MACDONALD JET WINGS 89

CHAPTER TEN   GROUNDED – NATIONAL SERVICE ENDS 103

CHAPTER ELEVEN   CHURCHILL'S MOST SECRET AIRFIELD 109

CHAPTER TWELVE   FLYING IN THE BLOOD 119

CHAPTER THIRTEEN FIFTY-YEAR REUNION 125

CHAPTER FOURTEEN THE FUTURE OF AVIATION 133

CHAPTER FIFTEEN NATIONAL SERVICE REVISITED 145

APPENDICES

   I Original National Service Bill 150

  II National Service Postings to the Armed Forces 157

 III Deaths in the British Armed Forces 1948–1960 158

 IV RAF strength 1959–62 + Service Numbers for RAF National Service . 159

  V The First Stages of Your National Service in the RAF 161

 VI National Service Bill 2013 163

VII Speech by Sir Baz North, KCB CBC ADS – President of RAFA 167

VIII The First Aircraft Flying Casualty 171

 IX UK Space Command 173

     BIBLIOGRAPHY 174

     ACKNOWLEDGEMENTS 175

FOREWORD

MARSHAL OF THE ROYAL AIR FORCE THE LORD STIRRUP,
KG GCB AFC

The Royal Air Force marked its centenary in 2018, taking the opportunity thus offered to reflect on its illustrious past and to set out its vision for a challenging future. In those one hundred years it had moved from an era of biplanes braced by wire to one of computer-controlled marvels flown by wire. These dramatic advances were very much in evidence during the centenary celebrations, which is perhaps no surprise for a technologically oriented service. Iconic aircraft, such as the Sopwith Camel, the Spitfire, the Lancaster, the Meteor, the Tornado, and now the Typhoon, have left their mark on both the RAF and wider history. However, the story of air power is not just one of machines. The people who flew and supported the aircraft were equally important; without their dedication, skill and courage our history would look very different. This book gives a personal, close-up look at one particular group of those people, of whom the author was amongst the last: national service aircrew. In doing so, it chronicles the close of an era and a system that enabled the contribution − and, indeed, sacrifice − of most of those who flew and fought for this country during the Second World War. It is thus an important record of a concept that was central to our national survival and to the freedoms we enjoy today. It also poses some interesting questions about the future of aviation in light of today's ecological challenges. However, above all it is a personal story about military flying, and about the human qualities necessary for success in that endeavour; qualities that are just as relevant and just as important to a modern air force entering its second century as they were to an embryo service operating flimsy biplanes over war-torn France in 1918.

FOREWORD

THE VISCOUNT TRENCHARD OF WOLFETON, DL

I am delighted and honoured to have been asked to write a Foreword to Lord Naseby's excellent book, which brings to life so clearly the days of National Service. More than two million young men were conscripted into the British Armed Forces to serve for two years from 1947 until 1963. Nearly one million of them chose to join the RAF. Michael Morris, as he was then, was one of the last to train as a pilot. I hope that you enjoy reading *The Few Who Flew* as much as I have.

Although I was too young for National Service, my childhood reading was, like Michael's, heavily influenced by the writings of Captain W.E. Johns. My grandfather is best remembered for his lifetime work in commanding the Royal Flying Corps in the First World War and then serving as Chief of the Air Staff of the RAF for some eleven years, firmly establishing it as a durable force which was capable of rapid expansion at the onset of the Second World War.

Michael's book shows clearly how much he gained from his service with the RAF, which equipped him well for his business career and in making the great contribution to Parliament that he has, both as the MP for Northampton South for twenty-three years and afterwards as an active member of the House of Lords. His love of flying and his deep understanding of aviation were kindled by his visits to Pakistan in his formative years. His knowledge of the Indian subcontinent and the circumstances leading to Partition in 1947 have informed his parliamentary work on India and Pakistan, and Sri Lanka, for which he leads the All-Party Parliamentary Group today. His work has made a significant contribution to building reconciliation in Sri Lanka following the end of the armed conflict in 2009. His thoughts about some kind of new national service, for one year, explored in the last chapter of the book, merits serious consideration.

Michael's story is a fascinating one and we are indeed fortunate that he has committed it to writing. I am very confident that the book's readers will be entertained, better informed and inspired by it.

INTRODUCTION

The Rt Hon. the Lord Naseby PC, formerly Michael Morris MP, Deputy Speaker in the House of Commons, was called up to do his National Service in late September 1955. He chose to join the RAF with the intention of becoming a fully-fledged RAF pilot and gain his Wings.

Ever since its initial formation, books have been written about the RAF and its pilots, but hardly any one, to my knowledge, has specifically focused on the young men who became National Service pilots. They were similar in age to those who Sir Winston Churchill immortalised with the title 'the few'; those brave young men who had flown and fought in the skies in the Battle of Britain and whose bravery, commitment, skill and fortitude were commemorated at the 80th Anniversary on Sunday 29 September 2020 at a special remembrance service, held in Westminster Abbey. It was this special event that provided the initial spark of an idea for my book, together with a very special poem, High Flight:

> Oh! I have slipped the surly bonds of Earth
> And danced the skies on laughter-silvered wings;
> Sunward I've climbed, and joined the tumbling mirth
> Of sun-split clouds, – and done a hundred things
> You have not dreamed of – wheeled and soared and swung
> High in the sunlit silence. Hov'ring there,
> I've chased the shouting wind along, and flung
> My eager craft through footless halls of air ...

The poem was written by a young Royal Canadian Air Force Officer called John Gillespie Magee who was killed in the Battle of Britain. He would have trained in the same skies in Canada as me, then Michael Morris, just fifteen years later. His poem – his legacy – perfectly captures the memory of the sheer thrill of flying and has particular poignancy as this book was researched and written during the time when the country, and indeed the world, was caught up in another epic conflict: fighting the Covid-19 pandemic.

CHAPTER ONE
ANOTHER BIGGLES

THE BLITZ HIT London in September 1940. At that time, my father was an architect and surveyor working for the Ministry of Works. One of four deputy heads, he was responsible for an area of southeast London which included much of the docklands. His job, night after night, was to go down to the stricken area caught in whatever raid had taken place, to work with the Emergency Services rescuing people and ensuring there was clear passage for ambulances and other rescue vehicles. It was a case of, 'shore up over there'; 'knock that down before it falls down'; 'get that burst water main isolated'. With his brusque but efficient manner, he was one of the many unsung heroes of the war, responsible for getting London and her inhabitants back up and running as quickly as possible, raid after raid. After the war, I remember him taking me to see his patch to show me the work he had done.

Our family – my father and mother, my baby brother and I – lived in a flat somewhere in Dolphin Square near the river in Pimlico. As the Blitz continued, the Germans moved their attentions to central London and their pilots used the Thames as a key navigational aid. It is therefore not surprising that the raids which were wreaking such havoc in the docklands would soon reach us in Pimlico. And so it was, on 5 November 1940, when I was very small, that there was a heavy raid which virtually demolished Frobisher House, near our flat. Apparently, when my father came home from work in the early hours, there was a quick family conference and it was decided that Mother, baby brother and I should be evacuated to a safer part of England. A few days later we were on a train to Bromyard, Herefordshire to stay as evacuees with a farming family called the Reids. I do remember getting on the train with a label round my neck, in case I was separated from my mother, clutching my gas mask, which were issued to all at that time.

The Reids were kind people and we settled into our one room, but the WC was at the end of the garden and the bath was a metal one positioned in front of the fire. No matter – many suffered more – but I recount this experience as it is one of my earliest memories and, on reflection, being caught up in an air raid with bombs destroying the place I knew as home, must have been my very first involvement with aircraft.

After the Blitz, we left Bromyard and moved to a flat in Tilehurst, outside Reading, for a brief time. Then Father found and purchased the freehold of a pleasant, detached house at 8 West Way, Pinner, Middlesex where life returned to some semblance of normal and I went to a pre-prep school called The Knoll. In autumn 1943, I moved to St John's School, Pinner, a proper feeder prep school which was closely linked to the Merchant Taylor's School, but not exclusively as I went on to Bedford School. My best friends, Charles Allen and Nick Coleman, went to Oundle and Bryanston respectively. We all wanted to be boarders.

St John's allowed us boys to be boys and it was not long before we were engaged in all the usual high jinks that schoolboys get up to, including designing paper darts. We were quite proficient, not just at making the traditional arrow-shaped paper dart but the broader more compact models too, complete with flaps capable of carrying a small bomb: a paper ball dipped in ink or an inner core of ink built into the dart itself. Perhaps our bombing raid experiences gave us these ideas.

We boys became experts at identifying the infamous Doodlebugs (V1 rockets). These rockets – or flying bombs – were unmanned and particularly deadly. At any given time, the engine would stop and signal to those below that it was about to plummet to the ground laden with explosives causing all kinds of destruction. I remember to this day, all too clearly, standing in the garden at 8 West Way hearing the sound of a Doodlebug approaching, looking up and seeing either a Spitfire or more likely a Hurricane tipping its wing so it would head for the countryside rather than the populated suburbs. The very mention of the word Spitfire is so evocative to so many. For me, it brings back memories of the Appeal Board, positioned in front of the library at the bottom of the High Street in Pinner, imploring the local community to raise funds for the building of Spitfires. At the top of Cuckoo Hill Road nearby, there was another large poster stating: 'Idle words Kill'.

My schoolboy imagination was also fed by the wonderful books by Captain W.E. Johns about the daring pilot Biggles. What a fascinating character James Bigglesworth was. He was a fictional character, based on W.E. Johns himself, but Johns afforded him a more dramatic and romantic personal history. Born in India in May 1899 (which is extraordinary, given my life-long association with India, its neighbouring countries and where I learned to fly), he joined the Royal Flying Corps in the summer of 1916 and achieved his first solo flight after just two hours of instruction. He was posted to France for active service in the First World War with 169 Squadron RFC and later 266 Squadron to fly the Sopwith Pup and the famed Sopwith Camel. At that time, he had under just fifteen hours of dual and solo flying time. It appears he had a 'score' of forty-nine aircraft, three balloons and one submarine, whilst he himself was shot down or crash-landed eight times. He was awarded the Distinguished Service Order and the Military Cross and Bar. By any yardstick this is an awesome record. Biggles was the ultimate hero, but I often wonder what sort of man his creator Johns really was. Reports show that under the stress of combat he developed from a slightly hysterical youth prone to practical jokes to a calm, confident, competent leader.

I still have some of the books I was given as a boy, which are now in the collection of my youngest son Jocelyn (aged forty-nine at the time of writing). One is signed by W.E. Johns – 'Biggles' himself – *Biggles Cuts It Fine*, which seems to be such an appropriate title for my dear, slightly rebellious, son. The true depth of my devotion and enduring fascination with these books is reflected in calling my own Jack Russell 'Biggles', a most devoted hound who follows me outside regardless of what I am doing in the garden come rain, snow or sunshine. For me, the most special book in the series is *Biggles in the Orient*, which was given to me for my twelfth birthday in November 1948. It reads: 'To Michael, with love from Auntie José and Uncle Harold'. They were not to know the relevance and importance of the word 'Orient' then, which one way or another, has dominated my life and had such significance.

During my last year at Bedford School as Head of Ashburnham's Boarding House 'Sandersons', I shared my study with an Indian boy called Kit Srinivasan. Later in life he was to become Head of India's Foreign Service. He would tell me about his home and India, and I was immediately fascinated by it. We spent many an hour talking about the repercussions of Partition, which saw the creation of the Muslim state of Pakistan and the Hindu state of India.

Then, in January 1955, my father announced that he had been appointed Chief Architect to the Punjab Government based in Lahore, Pakistan. Seven months later, as schools broke up for the summer holidays, I found myself, together with my two younger brothers Tristram and Crispin, on a P&O liner heading for Karachi. My lifelong association with this incredible, beautiful part of the world was just about to begin.

We three brothers shared a cabin and the journey took just under two weeks. Etched in my memory is Port Said, the entry point to the Suez Canal where the ship refuelled. We were not allowed ashore, so instead the local gully-gully men would bring their small boats alongside the liner and throw up baskets attached to lines laden with all sorts of delights they hoped we would buy. As our ship moved closer to the Suez Canal, the bartering became more and more frantic until eventually the gully-gully men could not keep up.

The sun was shining and it was very hot. The canal itself was amazing: narrow and flat on both banks and as our ship moved slowly through the water, it towered over everything on the banks below. It was here that I saw my first camel in situ, off the port side. Once through the canal it was full speed ahead for Aden, now a part of troubled Yemen. In those days it was little more than a trading colony on the shipping route to Australia. We did not stop long and were soon en route to Karachi, where Father was to meet us. As we approached the docking birth, I could see him standing next to his black Triumph with his bearer, Mustapha, alongside.

We set off for Lahore, which is about 765 miles northeast of Karachi. Father drove and Mustapha was chief guide, as he was the only person who could read or speak Urdu. My brothers and I were in the back. The journey must have taken at least three days with two overnight stops but my only recollection of it was our entry to the Sind Desert. We reached a T-junction in the middle of nowhere. Father asked Mustapha, 'Which way?' The response: 'Straight, Sahib.' I doubt Father kept calm but expressed words to the effect 'Mustapha, that's impossible, think again' – liberally laced with a few choice expletives as well. Anyway, the response was quite clear, 'Straight left, Sahib.' To this day my brothers and I laugh about 'Straight left'.

Lahore itself, whilst not the capital of the new Pakistan, was still the capital of the Punjab. I remember it as an attractive place filled with the bustle, noise and crowds of city life, dominated by its many mosques. My parents lived in a bungalow in a pleasant residential compound, and I still distinctly remember

The gully-gully men at Port Said.

The author in a Cessna.

Proud parents, Lahore, 1955.

our first dinner when my father announced to my brother Tristram and me: 'You two are going to have the opportunity of a lifetime; you are going to learn to fly.' Well, we were both dumbfounded and amazed! Indeed, we wondered what it really meant. Our father went on to explain that his assistant was a pilot and had found out that all British Government employees who had sons aged between sixteen and twenty-one, who held certain academic qualifications, could apply for their sons to be enrolled for a private pilot's licence. The reason was that the Pakistani Air Force was desperately short of pilots and this scheme was devised to boost its numbers.

So it was on the morning of 17 August 1955 that we two brothers were driven to the airport and introduced to Wing Commander Z. Ahmed. He explained the nature and duration of the course and what would be expected of us to achieve a private pilot's license. In addition to learning to fly, we would be expected to take part in ground lectures too. To round it all off, he said, 'Michael, you and I are going for a fifteen-minute spin.' We took off in a Cessna 140 Reg AP-AGE and did some gentle aerobatics whilst he pointed out some of the landmarks on the ground by which we would navigate, as well as some basic do's and don'ts. I was thrilled, captivated, excited and desperate to start. As soon as we had landed, I asked and was delighted with the answer: tomorrow morning at 07:30 hrs, to avoid the heat of the day.

From then on, it was full-time, five days a week, training and instruction. The day would usually start with a meeting with my instructor followed by external pre-flight checks, then take-off. There were eight of us on the course: six Pakistanis, my brother and me. We had access to two Auster planes and one Cessna, which was an altogether bigger plane and was used for longer flights. The Auster Aiglet was a Second World War spotter plane with high wings enabling a good view of the ground below. The plane had dual controls, so from day one I was mostly in control learning to handle the aircraft delicately through the control column. I believe even today I have sensitive fingers as a result of this training. After the flight, which lasted about forty-five minutes, there would be an hour-long lecture covering all aspects of flying, including air law, air safety, meteorology and navigation, as well as the mechanics of the planes we were to fly – in my case the Auster Aiglet.

The first challenge was to learn to take off straight without swerving all over the runway or even on to the grass and then to bring the plane down with a safe landing. This was relatively easy with a tricycle undercarriage of the Cessna but not the skid on the Auster.

On 26 August 1955, after eight flights totalling 5 hours 15 minutes' flying time, I was allowed to go solo. As I think back to it, I can still remember the nervous excitement as I completed the external checks of the Auster AP AFC, followed by the deep concentration I needed to really focus on every detail and procedure; double checking that the pitot head cover had been removed (otherwise the vital instruments would not have worked) and ensuring the take-off was smooth before allowing myself the biggest sigh of relief as I levelled the plane off at 1,000 ft.

This left me with a couple of precious minutes to think about how wonderful it was to be in the sky by myself; a feeling of complete freedom and exhilaration and time to enjoy the stunning landscapes that stretched out beneath me. But then back to the reality of having to prepare for landing and all the checks and procedures but in reverse order. It is difficult to emphasise the sheer thrill of returning safely to the cheers of my instructor and the ground crew. The family certainly celebrated on the Sunday at the Lahore Country Club, not least as it was the only day of the week that Worthington Pale Ale was served because of import restrictions caused by the weak balance of payments situation.

I had the most wonderful summer: flying in the mornings, most days, with the afternoons spent at the swimming club interspersed with rounds of golf. My dear mother ensured I saw all historical sites and gained a proper understanding of what had happened during Partition, as well as an appreciation for the Muslim religion and its sacred days, including Muharram when the true devotees flog themselves with a whip of several strands, causing their backs to bleed. Suffering comes in many forms, and it reminds me of an extraordinary sight in one of the large hangars at the airport. There were about a dozen small inter-war civilian planes seemingly in good condition lined up neatly in the hangar. Upon enquiry I was told these belonged to Hindu families who had to flee at the onslaught of Partition and their future ownership had not yet been determined. Just one example of the tragic impact of Partition.

As the summer progressed and I gained more experience, I found that particular high points for me were the navigation flights. They required a lot of work and I enjoyed the whole experience from the initial planning, seeking clearance from the air authorities, the map reading, anticipating the weather and getting agreement from my civilian instructor, a Mr Banash. On 10 September, we did one such excursion to Rawalpindi, a trip of some 200 miles. To fly at altitude whilst keeping an ever-watchful eye around the surrounding sky, and yet have time to take in the majesty of the scene below, is a truly wonderful experience. My logbook, which I have still have today, records the following:

Auster AP AFC, departing Lahore, 15.10hrs, arriving 17.50hrs.
12 September, same aircraft, leaving 08.00hrs, arriving 09.48 hrs.

We had booked to stay at the Country Club at Rawalpindi and were well looked after by the bearers whilst we mingled with some other aeronautical guests at the bar. It is incredible to think that I was just eighteen years old at this time and the amazing experiences I was having. Next morning, I took the controls once again and we landed back at Lahore after a flight of 1 hour 50 minutes. My appetite for further adventure was well and truly whetted by this trip. However, before I could progress further afield, I had to take the Radio Compass Navigation course leading to the 'A' licence test, which I took and passed on 14 September. I was now very conscious that this most wonderful episode in my life was fast coming to an end as National Service beckoned.

Whilst on holiday, having now outgrown the stories of Biggles, I had been dipping into a fascinating book on the early days of flying, recommended by my French teacher at Bedford School, called *Wind, Sand and Stars*. It had been written by a Frenchman, Antoine de Saint-Exupéry, who was one of the pioneer aviators who flew the mail routes to remote French African Colonies and to South America, particularly Chile, in the 1920s. His escapades included rescuing stranded pilots from rebel tribesmen. He was also an author of repute, writing *Night Flight*, which was awarded the Prix Femina in 1931. For him writing and flying had become two creative elements moulded together, and his writing, which with the help of my mother I read in French, certainly inspired me.

As my summer of flying was approaching its end, I knew that I wanted

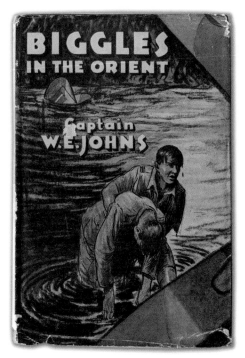

The author's inspiration: Biggles.

Flying records, Lahore, 1955.

my last trip to be a really worthwhile and memorable one. I had thought of somehow tracing the inhospitable border of Afghanistan which I had briefly seen on the return trip from Rawalpindi when I flew up to Peshawar. I talked it over with my boss, Wing Commander Ahmed, who liked the concept but said it was not very practical. He offered an alternative to fly down to Karachi International Airport, with a refuelling stop on the way at Multan, overflying Jacobabad. This would give a wide variation of topography as well the opportunity for seeing the heights of the Kirthar mountain range leading to Baluchistan as we approached Karachi and the Arabian Sea.

The deal was done. I set off with a more experienced pilot who was familiar with landing at Karachi International Airport, a Mr S.N.H. Naqui. He was kind and made it clear I was the pilot and that he was only there to step in in the event of a real problem. We chose the Cessna 140 AP-AGE, larger and capable of carrying four people – even though we were only two – but better equipped for the longer journey.

We were airborne at 06:35 hrs and arrived at Multan at 08:30 hrs. We took off again, overflying Jacobabad and seeing the vast Lloyd Barrage below – a low-lying dam which fed the surrounding areas. Then, on our starboard side we saw the majestic Kirthar Mountains, reaching up to meet us in the sky and in stark contrast to the flat plains through which the Indus River snakes and leads to Karachi. Mountains and rivers have always been, and will always be, such vital navigational aids. And very beautiful ones too.

On approaching Karachi, we contacted the control tower who asked us to do a circuit and come in behind an airliner that we could see on the opposite side of the circuit. I felt more than a tinge of excitement on final approach but succeeded to do a perfect landing before handing over the controls to my colleague Naqui, as he needed to be officially in charge on the ground. To this day I can remember elements of this very special flight, but the Karachi control tower sticks in my mind and watching the enormous airliner touch down ahead.

Just a few short hours later, I boarded a BOAC Constellation plane for my return journey to England; fortunately, I had a window seat in Economy. As the plane sat on the tarmac and then took off in the evening sun, I could not help wondering whether I would ever return to this magical part of the world. I looked out of the window as the aircraft banked and headed out to cross the Arabian Sea. I consoled myself with the thought that whatever National Service held for me, it would have to be in the Royal Air Force as a pilot. After all, I had my logbook listing my flying experience: I had gone solo after just 5 hours 25 minutes, and I had had the most magical forty-six days of flying. However, I also had what I hoped would prove to be a bit of an ace up my sleeve. Dated 21 September 1955, and which I still have today, a letter of recommendation from the Chief Flying Instructor of Lahore Flying Club:

> Mr Michael Morris joined the Lahore Flying Club on August 17th 1955. He went solo after 5 hours 25 minutes, since which he has completed all the specified hours for issue of his private pilot's licence and has passed all the examinations and tests. I consider his aptitude for flying markedly above average and should he so choose, I am sure he would have a very promising career in aviation.

> Signed: W. Banach

First Lieutenant Selfridge, US Army; the first recorded death in a military aircraft. (Wikipedia)

Orville Wright's crashed military flyer, 17 September 1908. (Wikipedia)

CHAPTER TWO
AVIATION IN ITS INFANCY

FOR THE GENERATION of British young men born between 1930 and 1939, the words 'National Service' had very great meaning, for they – or should I say 'we' – were 'conscripted' to give up to two years of our lives to the service of our country, almost regardless of individual circumstance. Given my extraordinary summer experiences, I returned from Pakistan keen for my own National Service to involve flying. This was in September 1955, and I can remember thinking and feeling that flying and aviation were still very much in its infancy: the Wright Brothers had made their first powered flight in Kitty Hawk, North Carolina in 1903 – just over fifty years previously. But such is the confidence of youth that I did not feel intimidated by the thought, but instead expectant and excited.

One day, I was discussing my research for this book with my daughter Susannah's friend, James Selfridge. He sometimes flies helicopters, but I can forgive him for that. Anyway, he said to me, 'I am directly related to Thomas Selfridge, who was the military passenger in the 1908 Wright Military Flyer trials on 17 September 1908.' Tragically the plane was overloaded and crashed. Selfridge fractured the base of his skull and died three hours later (the full, fascinating story is in Appendix VIII).

America and the Wright brothers really led the way in the early years of aviation, perhaps due to their natural pioneering spirit and an enduring commitment to their 'American Dream'. One must remember that for Britain, an island nation, the Royal Navy was the senior service and had been the dominant force to maintain the British Empire; the biggest empire the world had ever seen. So, at the turn of the twentieth century, the British Government did not really see flying as being central to her interests or in any way vital to our nation's way of life. Truth to tell, it was probably seen more as an expensive plaything for the wealthy elite – much more suited to the Americans than the English. It is fair to say, however, that the French had been trying hard in the Bois de Boulogne, and the Germans too, but their imagination had been captured by Zeppelins.

Thankfully, the English upper classes did contain a few eccentrics and entrepreneurs within its ranks, including the wonderful Lord Northcliffe, owner publisher of the *Daily Mail* newspaper. In 1906, inspired by the Wright Brothers, he came up with the idea for a competition – with a prize of £10,000 – to be awarded to the first person to fly an aeroplane the 185 miles from London to Manchester. This was the catalyst that Britain needed: it led to a flurry of activity in aircraft design and trial, and signalled the start of a number of air races, many of which included prize money donated by Lord Northcliffe and the *Daily Mail*.

Of course, the real game-changer for the development of aircraft came with the onset of the First World War. When war was declared on 4 August 1914, the Royal Flying Corps (RFC) was deployed as a part of the British Army. Reports show there were seven squadrons, although it seems only four were fully operational. It was not seen as an offensive force but instead its role was primarily to provide reconnaissance, and whilst the aircraft construction was robust, the pilots were inexperienced and the job was dangerous. In fact, most casualties in the early months of the war were due to crashes during take-off rather than from enemy fire. It seems that the army found its aviation arm sorely lacking and it turned to more reliable sources, namely balloons.

This reminds me of my French classes, aged fifteen, in the 'Removes form', called R3, at Bedford School. Our teacher was a wonderful Master called 'AGAH' properly known as A.G.A. Hodges. Mr Hodges had been a balloonist spotter in the First World War. The trick was to get five minutes into the French lesson and then put one's hand up and say words to the effect 'Sir, I was just thinking, did you learn all your wonderful command of French during the war when you were a Spotter?' Well, that was just the trigger he needed to spend the next fifteen minutes telling the class of his exploits. I can think of no other lesson that was half as enjoyable. It is probably the reason why my own French was never very good despite years of holidays in the south of France. The confusion was compounded by my having learned Hindi when in Calcutta – up to O Level standard – with the result that the Hindi and French now mould together and leave taxi drivers bemused the world over.

AGAH really was a delightful man in every way. When I left Bedford School near the end of July 1955, I called at his home but sadly he was out. He sent a letter all the way to Lahore dated 26 July 1955. I quote from part of it:

I'm so glad you have happy memories of R3. I have very happy memories of that form and I shall not forget you, for I must admit, I had a weak spot in my heart for you. But I've never known a boy who wasn't likeable. I love the school more than I can say. I shall never have the pleasure of teaching your sons, but I hope in course of time you'll send a crop of them to Bedford.

I did send two sons, Julian and Jocelyn, and a grandson, Oliver.

But I digress. The four years of the First World War saw an explosion of growth and change for British aviation; indeed, for aviation generally. However, things got off to a slow start for Britain, until late 1915, when someone decided to take charge. Thankfully, the right man came to the front at the key time: Colonel Hugh Trenchard.

In August 1915 Colonel Trenchard was appointed to take charge of the Royal Flying Corps. He had a clear strategy to achieve 'air superiority over the Germans'. It was his vision to extend the core range of aircraft and have a specialist fighter plane as well as a two-seater bomber, in addition to the reconnaissance planes. He also made the decision that each squadron would, if at all possible, just fly one type of aircraft and therefore become specialist in it. Furthermore, he was determined to break up the quasi-monopoly of design and production of new aircraft types by the Royal Aircraft Factory, which led to an explosion of interest from companies including Sopwith, de Havilland, Avro and others.

Of course, during this time the Germans were not sitting back and doing nothing; indeed, they attacked Britain with their Zeppelins. The first sortie was an attack on Great Yarmouth on the east coast in January 1915, which killed four people. This was followed by an attack on London in May. Although the Zeppelins seemed to be cumbersome and slow, it took until September 1916 to shoot one down; the pilot who did so, William Leefe Robinson, was awarded the Victoria Cross.

By the end of 1916 Britain had suffered a total of fifty-one raids, which had resulted in about 500 civilian deaths.

The last eighteen months of the war saw the Royal Flying Corps move forward in leaps and bounds and by the time of the Battle of the Somme there were a total of forty-seven squadrons with over 400 aircraft. Trenchard had achieved one his main objectives – to dominate the skies. But it came at a cost. Life expectancy of a pilot in 1916 was just ten weeks and by 1917 this number had dropped to just seven or eight weeks.

However, despite being some eighteen months behind Britain in its aircraft development, the Germans were never lacking in initiative and in 1917 they launched a new bomber called the Gotha G.IV; a huge aircraft with two engines and the ability to carry a load of seven 50 kg bombs. Moreover, they too had learned the art of squadron flying and were now able to formulate up to twenty or more aircraft to fly in formation and attack together. Indeed, one suspects but for the introduction of the Sopwith Camel, which brought huge advances to Britain's air defences, there would have been much devastation in London and other cities. There is no doubt that the Royal Flying Corps, its pilots and its aircraft, contributed greatly to bringing the bombing raids to an end in May 1918.

At the same time as fighter aircraft were being dramatically improved, there had also been developments in the organisation and deployment of the aircraft. A key initiative was the Strategic Bombing Wing, conceived to act independently, with none other than the now General Sir Hugh Trenchard as its commander. He had clashed with the Minister for Air, Lord Rothermere, and resigned from the Royal Flying Corps. But as they say, you can't keep a good man down, and we should be grateful for his enduring commitment to the aviation cause. The war ended on 11 November 1918. At its start, four years previously, Britain had less than one hundred aircraft and ended the conflict with around 23,000. The cost in human lives from this dangerous occupation of flying was 16,500 casualties and 6,166 killed in action.

As I researched this chapter and the Royal Flying Corps, which was to become the Royal Air Force, I found that Hugh Trenchard is justly revered as the 'Father of the RAF' by all who have served in the force, both then and now. He was a large man, both in stature and character, and had a loud, booming voice which earned him the affectionate nickname of 'Boom'. Again, through one of the quirks of life, it is a joy and privilege to sit on the Conservative Benches with the grandson of Lord Trenchard. His speeches are always thoughtful, well prepared and to the point; a credit to his grandfather, they are forcefully delivered and with characteristic booming.

CHAPTER THREE
THE PARLIAMENTARY GENESIS OF THE NATIONAL SERVICE BILL

W AR WAS DECLARED on 3 September 1939 and marked the beginning of six years of global conflict. As such, it is a date that is known and recognised by many. It is also a rather special date for me personally, as it is the date that I married Ann, in 1960, as well as being the date of the death of one of my personal heroes, Oliver Cromwell. It was also the beginning of the parliamentary saga which was to evolve into a series of National Service Bills, starting in March 1947 and continuing right up to 16 November 1953. These were relatively short Bills but would determine the fate of a generation of young British men, myself included.

The precursor to it all was the introduction of military conscription in April 1939 by the Conservative Chamberlain Government, bitterly opposed by the Labour Party. The irony is that eight years later, on 17 July 1947, it was a Labour Government which passed the first National Service Act by the same leaders who denounced Chamberlain. Even more ironic was the fact that Chamberlain's actions were deemed compulsory in time of war, but Attlee's were made in a time of peace.

As with most politics, it was not as black and white as it sounds. In fact, one must go back to first principles. The Labour Party did not oppose the principle of compulsory service in wartime but found peace-time conscription unacceptable. It had rejected Chamberlain's stance in the first half of 1939 when he had claimed the present situation was 'neither Peace nor War'. This was a claim made in the hope to win the support of Ernest Bevin, the Labour politician and founding General Secretary of the Transport and General Workers' Union (TGWU) who had supported the government's efforts to raise voluntary recruits. However, Bevin had made it quite clear that his earlier support was based on an assurance that compulsory service would not be introduced. Chamberlain found himself boxed in and on 29 March 1939 he announced that the government was still committed to voluntary service recruitment. It was said he was unwilling to introduce compulsory service because he needed the support of Labour. However, the very next month he changed his mind, and on 26 April he announced the 'Temporary and Limited' measures for the conscription of twenty year-old men for a period of six months' training.

Chamberlain found himself under increasing pressure for both diplomatic and military reasons: Britain had given guarantees to Poland, Greece and Romania to provide support in times of need and, additionally, the French Government had urged him to introduce conscription. In addition, the heads of the armed forces were advising of their concern at Germany's production of aircraft which could provide a knock-out blow to Britain. Chamberlain knew this meant Britain's air defence needed to be readied and, according to the Secretary of State, Leslie Hore-Belisha, this sealed the case for compulsory service: conscription.

However, Attlee did not go down without a fight and his memorable speech concluded 'the voluntary efforts of a free people are far more effective than any regimentation by dictators'. His concern went deeper, as he and others feared that National Service would lead to 'Industrial Conscription' with the spectre of destroying liberty. One might just reflect that Covid-19 and lockdowns come very close to what Attlee feared. What would he have made of them?

However, I digress and ought to record that pacifism ran very deep in the Labour Party of that era, although there were a few who did not share the same viewpoint, such as Hugh Gaitskell, a future party leader. Meantime, the Liberals under Sir Archibald Sinclair vacillated but, in the end, voted for the Bill, leading to 'The Military Training Act'.

It is interesting to see how public opinion changed with these vacillations. In January 1937 a poll showed only 25 per cent of the public was in favour of compulsory training. By April 1939 it had risen to 39 per cent, but by July it had reached 76 per cent in favour, as war must have now felt imminent and inevitable.

Whilst all these political and diplomatic negotiations and debates continued in the UK, Hitler took the advantage with the invasion of Poland, on 1 September 1939. Britain had been caught napping and the result was Chamberlain's Government being forced to hurriedly extend the call-up. This time it was with Labour's support. In May 1940, Chamberlain resigned and

Churchill formed a National Coalition in which Attlee and other key Labour players served for the next five years.

Ironically, it was Bevin who extended the wartime conscription to women, which saw them take up the jobs that the men had had to leave to go to fight. Labour ministers undoubtedly played a key role in mobilising the country for war. Later, as victory beckoned, they played a key role in preparing the country for peace too.

In the immediate post-war years, the biggest global challenge was the transition from war to peace, and the complex juggling act of balancing national security objectives with economic demands. In addition to this was the job of carving out new foreign and domestic defence policies which were often in direct opposition to each other: how could and should we support other countries as well as our own? There is no doubt that National Service also presented the 1945–51 governments with several difficult dilemmas. The central one was the allocation of resources between domestic and foreign/ defence policy objectives. We forget too easily just how disabled the UK economy and its finances were as the country went from one economic crisis to another, including the devaluation of the pound. It certainly did not help that the war had left Britain with military obligations which stretched across the globe.

In 1945 there were two issues over conscription. The continuation of the call-up in the immediate few years after the war and the idea of some sort of permanent conscription. There was not much support for permanent conscription. Britain faced enormous industrial shortages; the diversion of a productive workforce to the armed forces was hitting industrial production, the export drive and the balance of payments in a time when the country was facing huge financial and economic pressures. In addition to these issues were the more practical concerns of how long National Service should be and how many men could be accommodated and trained, to name just a few. However, whichever way the government and military chiefs turned, they came back to the same argument: conscription would lie at the heart of the future British defence policy, particularly for the army and the RAF.

The Air Ministry argued that 'Strong forces will be necessary to restore and preserve international order.' It estimated that it would need to train between 70,000 and 80,000 young men and they would be needed for two years in order to provide a robust and reliable air force fit for purpose in the event of a future global conflict. This period of two years would enable all ground personnel to complete the technical training and to be productive. For aircrew it would ensure full flying training with a short period of squadron service. (In my case it would have been five or six months with a squadron, but it was not to be with National Service coming to end in 1957 – but more of that later.) This was a huge commitment and the government was trying to respond to demands from all sides.

It soon became clear that regular recruiting, both to the army and the RAF, were running well short of requirements whilst Britain's commitments abroad were ever increasing.

In essence, conscription was inextricably linked to the pursuit of our foreign policy. It appeared to be the only way of having our armed forces at a level that would allow Britain to talk at the 'top table' of international politics. In effect it was a symbol of Britain's willingness to act to maintain our interests. And so, nearly two years after the war had ended and after many long and complex debates and much research, the British Government and politicians set about devising a suitable Bill to introduce National Service.

The National Service Bill 1947 (Bill 46, 1946–47) was printed on 12 March 1947. It was not a long Bill; just twenty-five clauses in thirteen pages and five schedules in a further eight pages.

It may help readers if I explain the life-cycle of a Bill. Every Bill must start its life in the House of Commons (unless it is truly not contentious). The first stage is the introduction, first reading and order for the Bill to be printed. Then there is time allocated for an important second reading, after which the Speaker puts it to the vote. If the vote goes against the Bill, it is dead. However, after a successful second reading, it goes to a committee stage where amendments can be tabled and voted upon. Once a committee has finished, there is a report stage where the amendments can be further debated and, if successful, incorporated into the Bill. The Bill is circulated for a third time and there is another vote in the House of Commons. If the vote is passed, it means it can go to the House of Lords. If it should be voted down, then the Bill is dead.

The House of Lords follows similar procedures as in the House of Commons, but on its arrival the Bill will be printed and its title will be read out in the chamber as a non-debatable motion, as its first reading. There is a long tradition that the House of Lords do not kill a Bill. Amendments can and are made by the Lords. If amendments are carried at third reading, the Bill returns to the House of Commons which can throw out the amendments. This going backwards and forwards can take place three times but on the third occasion the House of Commons can insist it does not want the amendment and the Bill passes without the Lords' amendment and it becomes law. In my experience of both Houses, which started in February 1974, there have been Bills, such as the Prevention of Terrorism Bill of 2005, which have not followed the norm. On that particular occasion, the House of Commons sat from 11.30am on Thursday 10 March until nearly 8.00pm the following evening of Friday 11 March, during which time the Bill went back and forth between the two Houses for a total of seven times – each time proposals and counter proposals to be considered. These exchanges are, to my mind, a classic example of the struggle between the two chambers of a bicameral parliament, in one of which the government had a majority but where the Opposition in the Lords had the power to destroy the Bill but was ever mindful of the possible political consequences of doing so. It is interesting to note that in the unlikely event of a tie, the Speaker of the House will vote for further discussion, if at all possible, following Mr Speaker Addington's example of 1796.

Returning to the National Service Bill of 1947: the second reading of the Bill took place over two days on 31 March and 1 April 1947. This is when the broad parameters of the Bill were debated with the usual vote at the end. The vote was carried out on the evening of 1 April with 386 voting Aye and 85 voting No: a handsome majority of 301 and by any yardstick quite substantial. After the general debate and first vote, it was referred to committee to explore the Bill in depth. In this case the debate on amendments took five days in a period between 6 and 15 May, finishing with the third reading on 22 May. It was then sent to the House of Lords where there were two separate second reading sessions on 3 June, followed by third reading on 2 July. The House of Lord's amendments were considered and accepted by the House of Commons on 17 July 1947. The reasons for the Bill were stated to be by the Minister of Labour, Mr Isaacs:

Primarily the need arises from the fact that the regular components of our forces have seriously run down because there has been no regular recruitment during the war... [A second reason] ... is the need for the nation to build up efficient, well-trained reserve and auxiliary forces.

The total period of service was to be eighteen months' full-time service and five and a half years with the reserves – in effect a seven-year commitment. Later in his speech Isaacs referred to the possibility that the eighteen months could be reduced to a year, which is in fact what happened. This may seem like a long time and a considerable commitment, especially today when life seems to be move so much faster, but at the time, the military leaders and armed forces deemed it to be insufficient. They were adamant that twelve months was totally inadequate, particularly for the RAF pilots who could not complete their flying training in that time.

For those interested, the debate makes fascinating reading and is available from the Historic Hansard website. By this time, Sir Winston Churchill was Leader of the Opposition, but still commanded the respect of the House, and I quote from his stirring speech, noted in the records as starting at 4.48pm:

On this occasion we support His Majesty's Government. We shall try to do so when they stand for national as apart from party interests and sectarian themes. We even go as far as to compliment them on the courage they have shown in resisting the subversive and degenerate elements in their midst.

Churchill was known for his impassioned speeches, but this has a different tone: it is respectful of the Opposition, which is rather refreshing. Certainly, in my fifty years in politics, I have seen great respect for the Opposition, on both sides of the House, although it might be noted that in the most recent times it has not been displayed in quite such abundance.

Later Churchill turned to address defence matters seeking information of the true strength of the Royal Navy, the army and the Royal Air Force. I quote:

Perhaps in the air there may be a little more mystery, because the air is a 'Kittle cattle' kind of service. Whether a Squadron is in the first line or second line or in training or in preparation and what is the exact grading of the various machines and pilots, all that affords an infinite field in which confusion may be created and statistics multiplied and spawned in vast quantities and varieties.

In his really powerful speech, he said near the end, 'We should have carried far more weight in the councils of peace if we had had national service.' He made one final observation that was pretty prescient about the future, namely: 'It is quite true that conscription for prolonged foreign service presents itself in a different light and cannot be maintained as a permanency.' There were a great many Speakers, the majority of whom have had military experience.

The final point to make is that the government also announced in the Bill that the National Service Acts would cease to have effect on 1 January 1954 unless a later date was to be fixed by Order in Council. This would mean that all young men born after 1 January 1936 would not be required to do National Service. On this basis I was not destined to do National Service but, thankfully for me, it was later extended to finish on 31 December 1957.

Although the Act that was passed stated that National Service full-time duration would be eighteen months, it did allow the government to reduce it to a year, which is what happened, following pressure from their own back benches and industrial leaders. Military leaders were aghast at the reduction, particularly as most of them had been lobbying for two years' service. Such is the nature of politics and democracy – you cannot please all of the people all of the time!

Twelve short months later – which would have added to those military leaders' argument that not much can be achieved in that time – it was clear that the international situation was deteriorating: there had been continual delays and disappointments in settling the final peace treaties following the war. Additionally, regular forces recruitment in 1948 had fallen badly. The net result of all this was a new, short Bill of just three pages and six clauses.

The second reading took place on 1 December 1948. All stages were completed by 14 December and the Bill became law, with National Service now at 18 months.

In March 1950, the new Attlee Government took over with Emanuel Shinwell at the Ministry of Defence who was known for, amongst other things, his doubts about National Service. Regular recruitment and re-engagement in the armed forces continued to be in decline.

He asked military chiefs to research the impact on the armed forces if there was no National Service. However, the exercise was barely underway when it was torpedoed by the start of the Korean War, which made radical reform unthinkable. To add to the worries of the impact of the Korean War, matters were none too rosy in relation to the Soviet Union.

The Air Ministry had been quick to make the case for National Service and had already reported that the RAF would have 300 fewer qualified pilots if it was discontinued. It continued to press its original case for a National Service of two years' full-time service followed by five years with a reserve squadron. Their case was strengthened by several senior Cabinet ministers lobbying the Prime Minister and encouraging him to be bold: not just with the developing Korean situation, but to reinforce the defences of Western Europe. One must give Attlee his due; he was not a ditherer. On 16 August he took the decision to extend National Service to two years and a week later he broadcast this decision to the nation.

It was now deemed vital that National Service should be used as a quasi-recruiting force for the regular army and RAF until such time that there was a clear reduction in Britain's obligations around the globe. Only when this was achieved could a fully all-regular armed forces be contemplated.

It was not until 1957 and Harold Macmillan's Government that confidence in the global situation had been restored and National Service could come to an end. By then, Britain's leaders felt buoyed by its strategic V bomber nuclear capability and had created a situation and opportunity where the country could return to relying on normal recruitment for regulars to staff all three services.

I think it is worth reflecting for a few moments on the impact of National Service, not least as all of us who were summoned to do it had been born before the Second World War and therefore had endured its devastating effects as young children. No less than 1.7 million men were called up to serve. The army led the way with 1,244,416 recruits, the RAF with 430,885 and the navy with just 43,583. The last soldier was demobbed in May 1963. It certainly ensured that the UK had trained forces at a time when voluntary recruitment would have fallen far short and could have exposed the country's weakness. Indeed, without National Service Britain could never have kept forces in the Middle East, Africa and Asia, nor attempt to revitalise the empire into the Commonwealth.

There were downsides, of course, the principle one being that at its peak in the 1950s it had a negative effect on British industry, which faced an acute shortage of manpower, affecting all sizes and types of businesses.

Personally, I felt the impact of the discontinuation of National Service soon after earning my Wings in March 1957. For instead of being drafted to a squadron I received my movement orders to report to 54 MU at RAF Hucknall just outside Nottingham, which did not even have its own runway! I also learned that my application to join the famous 601 reservist Squadron would be held in the pending file as there were rumours it might be disbanded altogether. Soon after I was offered a permanent commission in the RAF, but I declined as I had a place at St Catharine's College, Cambridge to read Economics. However, I get ahead of myself as my involvement with HM Forces only began at Catford, London SE6 in September 1955, but that is for the next chapter.

CHAPTER FOUR
CATFORD TO CANADA

THE WEEK AFTER returning from Pakistan I received my summons and instructions about signing on for my two years of National Service. I was to report to Catford, London SE22 Employment Exchange on Monday 27 September 1955 at 09:30 hrs. At the time, I was living with my grandmother in Forest Hill at the top of the hill above Horniman's Park. It was only a short bus ride from Forest Hill to Catford, but as it was such a fine morning I chose to walk down through the park and wondered what the next two years would be like.

I arrived in good time, received my ticket number and was told to sit down until called. I had filled in a form whilst still at school stating I wanted to serve in the Royal Artillery. I had been a sergeant in the Bedford School CCF and had taken a particular interest in gunnery. But following my flying experiences in Pakistan, I had changed my mind and I sensed it might be a difficult morning.

At around 11.00am my number was called so I went up to the relevant desk behind which sat an army sergeant. I can still remember quite vividly his opening remarks: 'Young man, this seems pretty straight forward; you asked to join the Gunners and it has been approved. In about a week's time you will receive a letter with your movement orders and a rail warrant. I wish you the very best of luck.' He evidently thought this was the end of the conversation but then I opened my mouth and said, 'Sir, I have changed my mind. I no longer wish to join the Royal Artillery but would like to join the RAF as a pilot.' The man behind the desk went bright red and said, 'You cannot do that!' I replied, 'Sir, I am quite serious; I have already learned to fly and wish to serve as an RAF pilot.' The stony-faced sergeant dismissed me with short shrift: 'You will go and sit over there and wait until I've seen everyone else before I hear more about this fairy tale. You may not leave this room until we have sorted you out.'

Fortunately, I had anticipated trouble, so I had packed a good book to read, and my ever-generous Grandma had given me a packed lunch. At around

2.30pm the sergeant came over and, in a kindly, enquiring voice, asked, 'Now what is this all about?' I explained about my visit to join my parents in Pakistan and that I had indeed learned to fly. I showed him my logbook with nearly fifty hours of flying time, as well as a record of my going solo after just a little over five hours' instruction. I also showed him my letter from the Chief Flying Instructor stating that I had an above average aptitude for flying.

After our initial exchanges earlier that day, I had expected some sort of adverse, explosive reaction, but, on the contrary, he was smiling. As he flicked through the logbook he noted the words 'Auster Aiglet'. He turned to me and said, 'You know, you could still join the Royal Artillery as they fly Austers as spotter aircraft but I suspect you would like something more challenging and maybe a bit of Squadron life.' He got up and advised me that he would have to contact HQ to get clearance, which would involve another wait for me. 'Not a problem, Sir,' said I. At around 4.00pm he returned and reported that it was all fixed: I would have to go to RAF Hornchurch for assessment. However, he pointed out, only two per cent of applicants get through. But then added, 'You might be lucky.' He told me there would be assessment tests and a medical and then I would be given a rail warrant to get to RAF Cardington. A few days later I would hear if I had been selected for aircrew training or not. Having been to Bedford School as a boarder, I knew exactly where RAF Cardington was, with its two massive hangers designed in the airship era. I rose, thanked him and set off home with a real jaunt in my step, letting myself be carried along by the happy thought that maybe I really might become a pilot: 'Biggles, here I come'. I also thought of my long-term girlfriend, Ann Appleby, who lived in Bedford and whom I had not seen since July. Maybe Lady Luck was on my side.

Later that week, true to the sergeant's word, a letter arrived telling me I was to report to RAF Hornchurch on Tuesday 5 October at 09:00 hrs for a two-day assessment. Hornchurch is not so far from Forest Hill, so I got up early, said goodbye to my wonderful grandmother and set off with all my personal possessions in one suitcase.

On arrival, we were all shuffled into a lecture theatre for a briefing on the two days and what they would involve, starting with a medical. I do not remember exactly how many we were, but I would guess it was about forty, and I seem to remember that we were broken down into four groups of ten. Understandably, the medical was exceedingly thorough. I came through it A1-G1. It was not all without incident, as the chap in front of me fainted at the sight of blood, which caused a slight hiatus and was possibly not the best start for him.

Two other activities stand out in my memory to this day. The first was an initiative test where each of us in the section had to take command for a specific task. My task was to get my team across a minor gorge. There was quite a lot of equipment lying around on both sides, such as timber planks, but all too short to stretch over the gorge. Thankfully, several years in the Cubs and Scouts came in handy as I remembered my knots. I decided the best course of action was somehow to get one of my team across to the other side, who could then use the really useful material on the opposite bank to help the rest of us across. I remember asking if anyone had gymnastic experience. As luck would have it, a lithesome young man put up his hand. We lashed two poles together which stretched across the gorge and my volunteer proceeded to get across hand over hand. He then lashed some long timber planks together and swung them across for us to build a bridge of planks. At the debrief at the end of the day we were told that only two teams had succeeded; I felt a warm glow of pride.

The other test was Morse code. We were each allocated a cubicle positioned alongside and facing a wall. It was explained that we were going to listen to Morse code. We were to put our headsets on so we could hear, and all we had to do was to record on our tapper when we heard a dot or a dash. The test would last around three minutes. The green light went on and we were live. Within a couple of seconds, I could see the chap next to me on my right tapping away. I tapped my headphone to make sure it was working but there was nothing, no sounds. After precisely thirty seconds there was finally a 'dot' followed by a series of dots and dashes, which continued for the next two and a half minutes. Later, I learned that this test was the one that caught out most students and caused them to fail: they were anticipating what they would hear rather than listening to the actual signal. This could be very dangerous in any real-life scenario and particularly when flying.

At the end of the second day, we were all called into the lecture theatre again. We were thanked for our co-operation and reminded by the Commanding Officer that we were the cream of the RAF National Service intake, so even if we were not chosen to be aircrew he was confident we would have fascinating and worthwhile ground assignments. I thought this was an encouraging message to take away.

After tea we went our separate ways and were ordered to reassemble a couple of days later at Bedford. We had been told to arrive at around 4.00pm, where we were met at the station and driven in a coach to RAF Cardington. We were shown our billet and then had dinner. I was so exhausted that I decided to turn in early: although it was only the beginning of October, it was bitterly cold, and the corporal in charge said the forces did not turn on the heating until 1 November. Wonderful! Then I remembered being told by my former Geography Master that Cardington held the record for having the lowest temperature in England; perhaps not so surprising as it was just about the midway point from the sea, be it west, south or east.

Next morning, we were up at the crack of dawn and at least the showers were warm. After breakfast we received a briefing on what we would be doing up until the weekend when we would disperse to our various postings. First drill: how to make one's bed, RAF style. Our billet corporal gave a demonstration under the eagle-eye of our sergeant. After the demonstration, all the bed clothes were ripped off and we were told we had fifteen minutes to make our beds, following which there would be an inspection. We set to with varying degrees of skill and enthusiasm. From memory, we were twenty in the billet. The sergeant and corporal returned and we were ordered to stand by our beds. Well, I think just two passed the test: some poor recruits had their bed sheets ripped off completely, others were bawled out for something or other. I certainly got into trouble because one of my pillows was not directly in line with the other.

Next, we were summoned to one of the hangers to be issued with all our RAF kit. However, we were told to be really careful with our clothing, as those of who were going to be aircrew would have to hand much of it back in. Lo and behold! on the third morning the notice came through who was selected for aircrew and who was not, and those who were, were ordered back to the hanger to trade in their boots for shoes. I was delighted that I was one of the few and I went to collect my new uniform with the greatest of pride. We were issued with different shirts and a No. 1 uniform, which included an officer's hat with a white band indicating, in my case, that I was now an Acting Pilot Officer. Thankfully, our corporal was now the epitome of sweetness and light to his young officers: we had made the grade.

The weekend was approaching and we had been told that on the following Monday we would be going to Kirton in Lindsey. I badly wanted to see Ann and so telephoned her from the telephone kiosk – after putting in some pence, as sadly there were no mobile phones in those days. I gave her the name and telephone number of the Commanding Officer, suggesting that her father might contact him to get me a 'Pass out'. Wonders of wonders, he was successful. Ann, her father and mother collected me from the entrance and we set off for a delightful evening at the Wheatsheaf in Colmworth. To this day, six decades later, Ann and I still visit this pub, so full of happy memories and now a restaurant called Cornfields, run by a good friend, Graham Goodhew.

In some ways I was sorry to only stay at Cardington for such a short period, as it has such an interesting history. In the 1920s, 1930s and early 1940s it was home to airships and there were several incidents involving them that stand out. In October 1930, the R101 was on its last flight to India when it crashed in northern France. The legendary musician and troop entertainer Glen Miller had been stationed at Bedford when his single-engine Norseman disappeared in fog en route to Paris in December 1944, never to be seen again. More positive stories include the development of the airship Airlander at Cardington, which continued until recently. However, as we set off in the RAF coach for Lincolnshire, I could not help but think a little about the R101.

Kirton in Lindsey lies 15 miles due north of Lincoln, just off the almost dead-straight A15. During the Second World War, Lincoln itself was well known to RAF Bomber crews, as the central tower of Lincoln Cathedral thrust through the low clouds and morning mists and would guide the Lancasters and others as they returned home from their bombing raids somewhere in Germany. We were going to a place that had a proud history and I was excited to be a part of it. I was in Red 1 Squadron – No. 71 Course, B' Flight.

I cannot remember exactly but it must have been about a twenty-week course, due to finish at the end of January 1956. I do recall it was bitterly cold the whole time as we were put through our paces, quite literally, with parade

The ill-fated R101, the pre-war queen of airships, above Cardington, Bedfordshire. (Air Historical Branch)

Where it all started: RAF Hornchurch. (Air Historical Branch)

ground training 'square bashing'. This seemed to happen almost every day. Our sergeant major must have served in the Middle East because when he felt we had done a particular movement poorly he would shout out, 'You gentlemen, don't even warrant a foreskin sandwich from Basra.'

Then there was cross-country running which I had managed to avoid at Bedford School, so I did not perform too well. However, I did do pretty well at the leadership exercises. Once again, there was the challenge of getting oneself and a team of five across a gap, but this time an icy cold canal, having first collected what we judged to be necessary from the station's scrapyard. Minus points if, according to the officer assessing us, we failed to bring a vital piece of kit.

We had classroom lectures covering meteorology, navigation and plotting courses which would have to allow for wind deviation and other challenges. Much of the classroom lessons involved a considerable amount of mathematics. My A Levels were in English and History, so I soon found my maths was lacking and, in fact, so rusty that I had to ask our lecturer for extra homework to help bring me up to speed.

Then there was night guard duty. Four of us, each armed with a rifle and five blanks, would be assigned to protect an Anson and two Chipmunk planes. It could be pretty eerie in the middle of the night. I remember exploring the Anson and sitting in the pilot's seat. Luckily, I resisted touching any of the levers, which is more than one luckless cadet in one of the courses ahead of us had done, causing the Anson's undercarriage to collapse. At the time, we took it reasonably seriously as we were well aware of the IRA, and they had already made a name for themselves by blowing up other military establishments.

We worked hard and we played hard, and I enjoyed my time at Kirton in Lindsey. There were Mess evenings which, though formal, were nevertheless sometimes quite riotous and although it was a competitive environment I made some good friends. Three in particular: the slightly mad Brian Stevens, known as Ginger, who had been in the air cadets at Tonbridge School; John Robbins, who had been brought up in Pinner where I lived until my parents went to Pakistan; and, finally, Tony Collins, who was possibly the most intelligent of we four. So, it was to no one's surprise when Tony won 'The Best All-Round Cadet' at our Passing Out Parade on 31 January 1956.

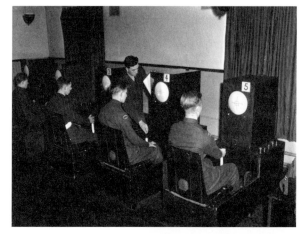

Testing reactions.
(Air Historical Branch)

Measuring for our No.1.
(Air Historical Branch)

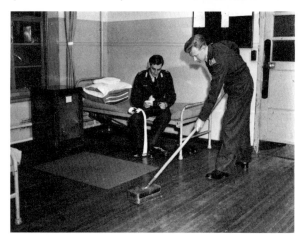

Bull night.
(Air Historical Branch)

Did we have any time off? I do not think we had any in the first month, as there was always something to do. There was also always lots of sport in which to participate, which I greatly enjoyed. Later in the course, I managed to get some thirty-six- and forty-eight-hour leave passes. The first I used to go to see my grandmother and to pick up my Vespa scooter, which was my pride and joy. This enabled me to visit Ann at her home and she reminds me that we would go to the restaurant Dujon in Bedford High Street, as it also offered dancing. Officially, her father banned her from riding pillion on my scooter, so to avoid any arguments she used to meet me just around the corner, out of the sight of her father, before climbing aboard. My other memory of the scooter was riding back to Kirton in Lindsey in the dark at a steady 40+ mph on fiendishly cold evenings with either rain or wind, and sometimes both, hitting me full on in the face, as the machine had no windshield. The last part of the journey was the 15 miles up the straight A15. When I got into my billet it used to take at least thirty minutes to thaw out.

The combination of hard work, good companionship and the camaraderie of Mess life left me buoyed with happy memories. Towards the end of the course, there was a degree of tension as we wondered where we might all be posted. Assuming we passed, and a few did not, we all thought we would be destined for one of the UK training schools like Little Rissington. But then another happy twist of fate changed my course: it had been decided that the course two weeks behind us would get to go to Canada to train. Apparently they were four short and so the powers in charge decided the top four in my course, Course 71, would go to Canada. To my frustration I passed out fifth.

Some hours after it was announced I was asked to see the Commanding Officer, who said, 'Morris, this could be your lucky day, as one of the top four does not wish to go abroad. Do you wish to go to Canada?' My answer: 'Sir, an emphatic, yes.' And it was done. The Commanding Officer dismissed me and wished me luck, adding that he felt I would make a fine pilot and officer. I thanked him for the opportunity. So ended my initial training at Kirton in Lindsey. Moreover, as our course had passed out two weeks ahead of the main Canadian course, we four were given an extra two weeks' leave. We would set off for Canada from Liverpool on 28 February 1956.

SS *Newfoundland* – our liner!

Our guide en-route to Canada.

CHAPTER FIVE
BOUND FOR CANADA

On 28 FEBRUARY 1956, the intrepid 'four musketeers' from RAF Kirton in Lindsey, No. 1 ITS Course 71, namely the new Acting Pilot Officers Collins, Morris, Robbins and Stevens, re-united after a month's leave, and assembled on the dockside at Liverpool. We were joined by eight other APOs from the course immediately after 71 to make up the new course 5517.

We had heard that some courses before us had flown to Canada in BOAC Boeing Stratocruisers. These were the state-of-the-art luxury planes with a bar on the lower deck. Rumour had it that one course had drained the bar of supplies whilst on the flight which, apparently, had been a first for the poor steward who had the misfortune to serve them. However, RAF policy had changed (I am not sure whether it was as a direct result of the aforementioned course's actions or not) and it was thought preferable that officers should travel by sea in one of the modern, post-war liners like the RMS *Empress of England*. Since none of us had been across the Atlantic before, the whole prospect was one of unmitigated excitement.

Imagine our surprise when we learned that there was no smart liner for us, but instead an ocean crossing in the SS *Newfoundland*, a Furness Withy Liner of just 7,500 tonnes – most liners in service at that time were between 15,000 and 20,000 tonnes. Before leaving home I did a little research and what I found did not augur well. The first SS *Newfoundland* had been built in 1872 and was a sealing ship. She came to an uncomfortable end and was wrecked in 1916. The next SS *Newfoundland* was launched in 1925. In September 1943, she became HMHS *Newfoundland* to be used as a hospital ship for the Eighth Army. She was sent to deliver a very precious cargo of 103 American nurses to the Salerno beaches. On her arrival there, on 12 September, she was attacked by dive bombers, not just once but twice. That night the *Newfoundland*, together with two other hospital ships, were moved out to sea to anchor for the night. All three ships were brightly illuminated and carried standard Red Cross markings to identify them as hospital ships, which should have afforded them protection under the Geneva Convention. However, at

5.00am the following morning, 13 September, the ship was hit by a Hensel Hs 293 air-launched glide bomb from a Dornier Do 217 belonging to KG100 squadron. The ship was badly hit, caught fire and despite the best efforts of the crew it was clear she was beyond repair, so the decision was taken to scuttle her the next day. Certainly not the happiest history but I decided to keep quiet about it, as I did not want to dampen morale and we were all anticipating a lovely voyage to Halifax, Nova Scotia with a brief stopover at St John's, Newfoundland. But however hard I tried to liken it to my cruise to Pakistan with P&O, I could not get the fact out of my head that that had been in mid-summer and this was late February.

However, we each strode up the gangway, excited about the year and a bit ahead. The exhausting work at Kirton in Lindsey was behind us and I like to think we each had a fair bit of confidence: we were to train to fly the Harvard and then the T33 Silver Star which would, in time and all being well, earn us the highly-coveted 'Wings'. As we set sail and approached the open sea we found a sheltered spot under the overhang at the stern. The ship began to roll a bit, but we thought little of it as we headed down to find our cabins – from memory they were quite pleasant, with just two sharing – before we had dinner. It was starting to rain by now and we decided to retire, our stomachs starting to churn. We all slept well and had agreed to meet the next morning under the awning in the fresh air before going in for breakfast. By which time, of course, we were somewhere in the Atlantic and the ship was being hit by great big Atlantic rollers which caused her to plunge down one side of a huge wave and up the other side, twisting as she went. We bravely tried breakfast, but no one could take anything cooked. During the day, it was all we could do to stay in our locked-down chairs, huddled in our duffle coats. I cannot remember exactly how long it took to travel across the Atlantic, but it seemed a like a very long voyage indeed. As Robbins described it, we were all 'mal de mer'. Later we were told it was the roughest crossing the Newfoundland had made in years. Boy-oh-boy were we glad to dock at Halifax, Nova Scotia.

Once we had docked at the quayside, an RCAF Officer came aboard to welcome us and give us a short briefing on what was in store for us in the coming weeks: we were to set off the following morning by train for London, Ontario. There we would have a short, three-week course involving various briefings about RCAF Moose Jaw where we would start our training,

Saskatchewan for Harvard piston engine training, then jet conversion on T33 Silver Stars at RCAF MacDonald near Winnipeg, Manitoba. We would be meeting up with all our NATO colleagues from France, Belgium, Holland, Norway, Denmark, Turkey and later our Canadian cousins too. Canada, under the newly established North American Treaty Organisation, had agreed to train a significant number of pilots and navigators as part of its contribution to the organisation, rather similar to the former Second World War Commonwealth Air Training Plan. We were told our training would also include lectures on Canada and Canadian life. The officer concluded by handing out a 'Welcome to Canada' booklet, adding that our course would be shorter than for the other nations as they needed to improve their English. So, once we had completed the introductory two-week course, we would have leave to see a little of Canada and, if we liked, we could go over the border to the United States and even visit New York! We were so excited! To cap it all, he announced there was a local dance that evening to which we had all been invited, with transport laid on, providing us with an opportunity to sample some Canadian hospitality and dance with some attractive young Canadian girls. The trials and tribulations of the cold, bumpy Atlantic crossing faded away and we were much cheered.

At 7.00pm local time, we hopped into a bus, I think in uniform, but full of anticipation for a fun evening out. On arrival at the dance hall, we went to the bar to order our drinks which were on the slate (to a limit). The barman asked John Robbins, 'You are twenty-one, sir?' 'Yes,' replied John, showing his ID. This was incredibly lucky, as the rest of us were only nineteen! And so it was that for the duration of our stay in Canada, dear John always had to do the ordering. We could hear the music playing, so we went into the hall to find a few couples dancing. John got up and said he felt like a dance, picked out an attractive young lady, walked over and asked her if she would like to dance. With no hesitation she said, 'No,' and he returned crestfallen, shaking his head. We teased him a little, and then Tony and I tried but met the same fate. Only later, when talking to a couple of young ladies did we learn that their mothers had told them in no uncertain terms to stay away from the RAF Brits, as they were only in town for one night.

Next morning, we caught the train heading for RCAF London, Ontario, watching the St Lawrence River pass by with all its shipping. It turned out to

Lifeboat drill. Photo taken by John.

Wrapped up in our duffle coats.

be a longer journey than any of us expected. I suppose we had no real idea of the size of the country: Canada is huge. Once we arrived at RCAF London we were not very impressed, as the accommodation was pretty poor; a large barrack-type room with about twenty bunk beds and the other students had already bagged the best ones, such as they were. But we were there to work and we set-to, starting with an intensive two-week course conducted by the NATO Training & Induction School. It familiarised students with RCAF aircraft and its terminology, flight procedures, meteorology and basic navigation, not to forget the inevitable medicals. We were each given a little booklet 'RCAF – OFF to Canada' with lists of the 'do's and don'ts' but there was nothing on the subject of how to ask a Canadian young lady for a dance!

Those who spoke English were then free to go on the promised week's leave, whilst those who did not were required to stay for another intensive course to learn it. A few suggestions were made about where to go and top of the list, and therefore our first excursion, was to the Niagara Falls, one of the Wonders of the World, and rightly so.

We four Brits had followed the tourist trail taking us to the top side of the falls in all their magnificence. Brian and I decided to walk down the Canadian side to get a closer look of the edge of the falls. About halfway down we noticed what seemed to be a path leading directly into the rock over which the water fell. There was no notice advising us not to enter, so we went forward and found ourselves virtually in the middle of the falls, with a balcony jutting out as water cascaded down at a huge speed. There was ice everywhere. Undeterred, we stepped out on to the flat ice a little way and felt the full powerful strength of the falling water. I can still envisage it to this day: it was simply awe-inspiring. Only later, when we saw a picture postcard of the tunnel did we realise that we had walked way beyond its end and on to a mountain of frozen spray.

The second adventure was a trip to New York, to which none of us had been before. We had been told that the best way to get to it (and certainly the most economical) would be to hitch-hike, in pairs and in uniform. We decided to give it a go and made plans to meet up at the YMCA hostel in the city, which we had booked for a stay of three nights. The hitch-hiking was actually really easy, as people were friendly and helpful: no doubt the uniform helped. We made the journey in one day and met up at the YMCA as planned. It has to be said that the accommodation was really very basic, even more so than at RCAF London, but no matter: we were young men and keen for adventure, and we were only staying a few nights.

I know we went to see a Broadway show but I do not recall what it was. However, I do remember a rather special visit to the Federal Reserve Bank of New York facilitated by David Cobbold, another RAF APO, whose father was Governor of the Bank of England. What a visit for us young aspiring pilots! We were shown to the office of the bank's President, some hundred floors up with a view down to street level. The view was incredible. It is easy to forget that this was in a time before mass media and the internet, and we could not conduct a quick google search to bring up images from around the globe. We did not have skyscrapers in England and so the view from the top of one left us as awestruck as the view of the Niagara Falls. Of course, banks, even big ones, are not famous tourist attractions and there is one place in particular that is never open to the public: 'Would you like to visit the vaults?' asked our host.

We descended to below ground to what felt like the centre of the Earth, surrounded by solid rock, and came to the door of the vault. Some 5 m in diameter, it required the presence of several top bank officers to be opened. Once we were inside it was immediately closed behind us. What a sight! Gold bullion from floor to ceiling, divided into cages with the names of the countries whose property it was listed on the cage. 'If you can take one of those ingots without me noticing, you can keep it,' said our host. Ginger accepted the challenge and with both hands and much difficulty he managed to lift a small part of Argentina's gold reserve. Reluctantly, he agreed that it should stay put.

A visit to New York would not be complete without a trip to the top of the Empire State Building which, at the time, was the tallest building in the world. The views were impressive but somehow not quite as impressive as our views at the bank – from both above and below ground. We also visited the United Nations headquarters and enjoyed seeing many of the conference halls, although not in session, and were allowed to walk freely wherever we wished. A trip to the Rockefeller Center completed our visit to the Big Apple.

There were two other trips arranged to Toronto and Detroit, but I do not recall going on either. The consensus was that we had thoroughly enjoyed ourselves in our week off but now it was time to return to RCAF London, ready to move to RCAF Moose Jaw by train.

At this time, London, Ontario was considered to be the cultural centre of this part of Canada, yet it was located in the middle of the country's industrial heartland. We had also been told it was the centre of the insurance business and home to the University of Western Ontario. There seemed to be as many Americans in London, Ontario as Canadians, but as we were only stationed there for a few short weeks, we did not have time to really get to know it and find out about all that it offered.

We boarded the Canadian Pacific Railway, Trans-Canada Express for the 2,500-mile single-track journey to Moose Jaw, Saskatchewan in the heart of the Prairies. The train's ultimate destination was Vancouver on the west coast. The train had observation compartments above the sleeping accommodation so we could take in the scenery as we moved forward at a leisurely 40 mph.

The train wound through northern Ontario; a scene dominated by trees,

Farewell dinner menu, SS *Newfoundland*, 9 March 1956, signed by those present.

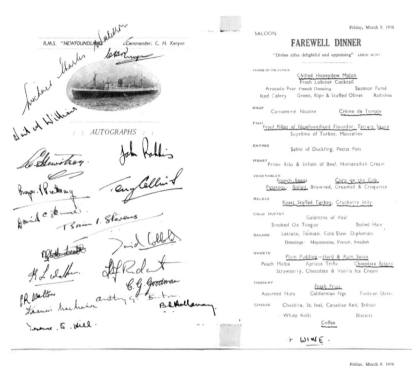

Farewell dinner menu, SS *Newfoundland*, showing all the signatures.

lakes and rivers which then repeated itself with more trees, lakes and rivers. The following day it was trees, lakes and rivers again, until suddenly in the evening the domed express bent around the corner and there, before the traveller, was the red ball of the evening sun dipping into the blue expanse that is Lake Superior. The north shore of the lake is cut and scarred with rocky inlets and miraculously the train follows its contours. At the end of the lake the train turned west and gradually the tress, lakes and rivers were left behind, until at Winnipeg the Prairies began. Winnipeg is a large city in the Prairies, in fact the last city of any appreciable size until you reach the far end of the Prairies at Edmonton or Calgary. However, our destination was Moose Jaw, right in the heart of the Prairies. For the next few hours, the land we passed was dead flat, sown, in the main, with wheat, but at this time, for as far as the eye could see, was a winter wonderland, covered in a blanket of snow.

We arrived at Moose Jaw on 1 April 1956, a town of just 25,000 people with little claim to fame, although several years later I learnt that it was the bolt hole of Al Capone, given its proximity to the US border. We climbed down from the train and watched it depart again, with its Canadian 'hoot' that we would learn to love every day. We boarded a bus with all our gear and headed out of town to the south. The first landmark we saw of the air force base was the control tower that juts into the sky. We disembarked and were shown to our room. Thankfully, it was in a modern block and really quite pleasant and, better still, we four were all together. We gave a sigh of relief that we had arrived safely. This would be our home and life for the next nine months.

My love of trains – the Canadian Pacific engine.

Wrapped up to face the
Canadian winter.

En route to RCAF London
Ontario.

Niagara Falls.

CHAPTER SIX

RCAF MOOSE JAW – EARLY DAYS

THE TIMING OF our arrival on Easter Saturday, 1 April, was near perfect, as most of the winter snow had gone, except where it had been piled up in heaps to clear paths, etc, and it was a glorious day with the sun shining. The four of us – Collins, Robbins, Stevens and I – were to share a room and from our window we could see the runways and all the activity on them. The first task was to agree who slept where. I was not fussed and ended up nearest the door. The room was comfortable and we each had our own cubicle of bedside table and wardrobe with two beds along one side and the other two positioned opposite. We also had our own bathroom and, wonder of wonders, we were issued with a steam iron, which was virtually unheard of back in the UK at the time and felt rather high-tech. However, as we had to do our own laundry, including ironing our RAF shirts, it was a welcome and necessary piece of kit. Thankfully, one of our group soon realised that for shirts we really only needed to iron the bits that showed; namely the front, collar and cuffs, which saved each of us a good deal of time.

Once we had unpacked, we were invited to a lecture by the Commanding Officer, welcoming us to RCAF Moose Jaw 2FTS (Flying Training School). There were eight nations taking part under the auspices of NATO: Canada, the UK, France and Turkey were represented by ten cadets each and Norway, Denmark, Belgium and Holland had four cadets each, making a total of fifty-six cadets. This is no small number, particularly when one reflects there were three other courses ahead of us at 2FTS. The Commanding Officer started with some basic geography to familiarise us with the local landscape: we were right in the centre of the Prairies, the wheat bowl of Canada. To the south of us was the international border with the USA, which in flying time was less than five minutes away, 'so beware' warned the Commanding Officer. Although Moose Jaw was the fourth largest city in Saskatchewan, it had a population of under 20,000. I could understand that because as we had been driven from the train station the place seemed to me to have just one main tarmac road through the centre which soon changed to dirt roads on

RCAF Moose Jaw: author with our 1940 Dodge.

RCAF Moose Jaw roommates, left to right: Ginger, Michael, Tony and John.

NATO friends with Tony and author.

the outskirts. But the Commanding Officer reminded us that not only was it served by the Trans-Canada Railway but also by the Trans-Canada Highway and there was a daily Dakota from Canadian Pacific. So we were not cut off at all and, he added, slightly tongue in cheek, that we should not ignore the Moose Jaw River (although it was not really navigable).

The Commanding Officer continued by explaining how our time would be filled: for the first week, half the course would receive lectures in the mornings whilst the other half received aircraft instruction on the ground and then we would swap in the afternoons. Flying would only happen from the end of the second week. He emphasised the weather could change very rapidly at Moose Jaw, with snowstorms in the winter and violent thunderstorms in the summer. With any extreme weather, there would be no if or buts, and all aircraft would be ordered to return to base immediately. He finished the lecture by inviting us all to a special evening drink and dinner to welcome us. For us on course 5517, which is how we were known, the training split neatly into two halves. There would be four months of learning to fly, then a two-week summer break, followed by three months of intensive training to learn how to fly and manage an aircraft in all sorts of situations, including night-flying, formation flying and some serious aerobatics.

The first two weeks were spent in the classroom, and we learnt about all aspects of flying, with particular focus on the Harvard MK II plane. There were regular exams that had to be passed. However, all the questions had multiple choice answers. When the NATO scheme was set up, it was clear to those designing the course that English would not be first language for some of the cadets and so multiple-choice answers were seen as more appropriate.

Whilst these two weeks were mostly spent engaged in academic study, we did also go into the hangars to see, touch and begin to get a feel for this unique aircraft: a tough trainer all painted in yellow with the RCAF Roundel and the Canadian maple leaf. In addition, there was plenty of physical exercise in the gym. I have my logbook in front of me as I write. I note that on 25 April I signed what is headed 2 FTS Flying Orders Appendix C. The heading is 'Certification'. It reads:

I have read and understood CAP 100, Station Standing Orders and 2 FTS Flying Orders.

I know the location and limits of the local flying and Practise Forced Landing Area.

I have been instructed on and fully understand for the Harvard MK II and IV.

These were all the things I had to know and have experienced before being allowed to be either a pilot, or first pilot or second pilot. In addition, we were taught and were required to have a thorough understanding of the brake and fuel systems, engine operational limits, method of recovery from spins and unusual flying conditions, as well as how to deal with a number of specific emergency situations.

RCAF Moose Jaw provided us with a full timetable and there was little or no room for external activities. However, the Mess and bar were good, so after a long day it is where we tended to repair for the evening. However, all of us on Course 5517 were banned for a week after our dear Norwegian colleagues, who were celebrating some Norwegian event, got absolutely sloshed and decided to throw their empty glasses over their shoulders into the fireplace. They caused total havoc and there was broken glass everywhere. The bar steward immediately called the Military Police, resulting in all 5517 being thrown out and subsequently confined to barracks for a number of evenings.

At last life as a pilot really began for me on 10 April. Looking back, it was only ten short days after our arrival at Moose Jaw, but for us young bucks it felt like an age. My instructor, Flying Officer Stewart, had run cockpit drill which took four hours on consecutive days, but it was completed in time for my first flight in a Harvard, which my logbook describes as a familiarisation trip lasting just one hour. Of course, I had flown nearly fifty solo hours in Pakistan but that was on the docile Auster Aiglet and Cessna 140, not the Harvard beast which was altogether a much more challenging task. I had to wait another twenty-four hours before I would have the controls again, and only for part of the time, under the instruction of Flight Officer Stewart. But there followed six consecutive days of intensive flying training, starting with circuits and bumps (landings).

Looking at my logbook, I wrestled with the various tasks and manoeuvres,

Harvards in
loose formation.
(William March)

NATO friends in mufti with Tony, John and author. (Brian Stevens)

5517 Red and Blue Flights.

Harvards awaiting the
cadets on the tarmac.
(William March)

Ginger records his flight plan.
(Brian Stevens)

Mid-summer uniform.
(Brian Stevens)

Harvards over the Rockies.
(William March)

all allocated a number. One could not progress on to the next number until the previous one had been completed properly. That week, I moved steadily through numbers one through to eight.

But what do I really remember? Firstly, I remember walking out from the hangar, proudly carrying my parachute before completing my external checks. I would then double-check the cover had been removed from the pitot head, otherwise the instruments would not work. The ground crew would always be present, as they were part of the starting procedure and so I made sure to have a quick chat with them: perhaps it was the nascent politician in me, but even then I appreciated the important work they did to enable us pilots to get up into the air. Then, round to the port side to carefully climb up the wing and into the cockpit. I would make sure my parachute was comfortable, fix the straps and connect the radio. My instructor would be in the rear seat, checking every move. When we were both ready, he would give the sign to start the engine and if all was well it was 'chocks away' and we would taxi out. There cannot be a more difficult aircraft to take off – and perhaps it is used for training for that very reason. A pilot cannot see straight ahead so has to zig-zag to see where he is going. Once we had reached the end of the runway we had to wait for clearance for take-off. Then, open the throttle, slowly, to full. Ever mindful that the Harvard has a pull to the left which would take us on to the grass, I had to use the right rudder. The tail went up and at last I could see where we were going. I checked airspeed and gently eased the stick back and we were airborne. Truth to tell, I did not visit the grass very much, but watching others I felt that their instructors must have had a few grey hairs.

The next challenge was to go solo. I had my PCH test for solo on 26 April. This was the name of the Canadian equivalent of the pre-flight checks. As I remember, this was followed by my instructor climbing out and wishing me 'Good luck'. I taxied to the end of the runway, awaiting clearance from the tower. The voice then came, 'Aircraft 20399 you are cleared for take-off.' What a sensation and thrill! Within a few seconds the tail was up and a few more moments later I had take-off. Wheels up, turn to starboard, parallel with the runway and looking carefully around, I radioed the tower who requested me to do a full circuit and then land. No problem! I even had time to look around a little – there really is nothing like the view from an aircraft. But all too quickly my circuit was complete: I got clearance to land, made a reasonable approach

A pretty good
fly-past.
(William March)

A thumbs up
from the author.

Author at the
ready.

A prang. (RCAF).

Our NATO colleagues. (Brian Stevens)

Busy days.

Ties cut after going solo – author fifth from left – one of the first.

and then the wheels touched down just beyond the numbers. It may have been a little too fast, but all safely done. I taxied in, parked the aircraft and checked everything was switched off before pulling back the canopy and jumping out to the encouraging sounds of 'Well done, Sir' from the nearest member of the ground crew. My instructor said, 'Morris, 8 out of 10' and I was elated.

Going solo is such an important part of flying life and it was duly celebrated in the bar that evening. In the tradition of these things, my black service tie was cut off below the knot whilst I was standing. Then, with coloured chalk, it was inscribed with a Union Jack at the top, underneath the letters MORRIS were written vertically down the tie, with RAF horizontally and underneath, the date: 26 April. I do not remember any more of the evening except that when the bar closed I had to be guided back to our room. As I sit here typing, tie in front of me, I suddenly realise this happened sixty-five years ago, almost to the hour.

From that day on, I flew six days a week to work my way through manoeuvres numbered twelve, right up to the final, number twenty-five. For some strange reason I had two flights with a Harvard MK IV with a different instructor, Flying Officer Simons, but there is little to note in the difference between that and the MK II. By the end of May, I had clocked up a total of 30 hours 50 minutes of dual flying time and 13 hours 15 minutes of solo flying time. As spring turned to summer, the hours, like the temperature, continued to rise so that by the time my leave began, on 17 August, I had a total of 61 hours' dual flying time and 49 hours' solo. The last three days before my leave began, my logbook records 'G.F. Revue' which I take to be the review of my performance thus far. I was conscious that Flight Officer Stewart was not pushing me hard enough. I was confident of my instrument performance: I had completed the drills whereby a hood is put over the cockpit so a pilot cannot see and is forced to make a landing purely on instruments, but my aerobatics even in their simplest format were not good. We had been informed that in the summer break there would be a review of every cadet and changes must be anticipated.

However, summer leave beckoned and so, together with my three British roommates who were now dear friends, I set to cleaning up and readying a new shared purchase: a 1940 blue and white Dodge. We had clubbed together and bought it for the princely sum of $120. We had grand plans and were about to hit the United States.

CHAPTER SEVEN
SUMMER LEAVE

AFTER FOUR MONTHS of concentrated training involving flying every day, sometimes twice a day, plus classroom lectures, we four musketeers were ready for our summer break. At the end of a normal full working day, we four – Tony, John, Brian and I – loaded bags into our newly purchased blue and white 1940 Dodge car in preparation for a fortnight's tour of western USA and Canada. To be honest, at the time we were a little bit worried about the condition of the clutch, plus there was an unhealthy rumbling coming from the big end bearings. We thought about repairs, but we were young and carefree, and the consensus was to get as far away from Moose Jaw as possible that evening and we would worry about repairs later.

We left camp at 6.00pm and set off for Swift Current where we planned to spend the night. We quickly adopted our tried and tested routine when driving as a four: we each drove for one hour; the front passenger would navigate and the two in the back would rest. Thanks to the Dodge having a cruise control button, we actually devised a unique hand-over system: at changeover we would set the hand throttle knob, the driver would move to his right while the passenger next to him would climb over to the back. The chap behind the driver would climb into the front. Once everyone was settled, the new driver would disengage cruise control and take over. We became really rather adept at this manoeuvre.

The weather that evening was very poor. Earlier, it had been raining steadily, making the road quite slippery. Tony was driving when we passed an overturned car in the ditch and he recognised it as our fellow training pilot and friend, Dave Edgar's Plymouth. We immediately stopped and were told that the accident had occurred only very recently. All the occupants were on our course at Moose Jaw, including our RAF colleague Terry Hill. Only the driver had been hurt and had been taken to hospital; by some miracle, the others had escaped with bruises and had gone off in a police car. We went to the Herbert Hospital and were told Dave's condition was critical. The others soon arrived but we waited until they had given their statements

Summer leave in USA.

Putting the Dodge through its paces.

The Old Faithful geyser erupting.

before giving them a lift to Swift Current where we all spent the night.

The following morning we said cheerio to Terry and the three Belgians who had been in the accident and headed south to the border with the US. First, we had contacted the hospital and had been reassured that Dave would be OK and that he would be returned back to Moose Jaw on discharge from hospital. The roads were terrible and, if anything, they deteriorated after crossing the American border. Our first stopping place was Malta, Montana where we had lunch and bought a tyre which replaced one that looked fit to burst. While we were looking round the town, we were accosted by an American border policeman and spent a most embarrassing ten minutes trying to persuade him that we were not in fact smugglers but just four RAF officers on legitimate leave. Eventually we got away and motored across the prairies and cattle land. Our next stop was at Havre, where we bought a few souvenirs and postcards. One peculiarity was that the traffic lights emitted a loud squeak every time they changed colour! I am not sure if it was deliberate or just an ageing piece of machinery. Either way, it was the only impression I took with me from Havre.

We decided to take the road to Great Falls, where we hoped to arrive that night. En route we only stopped to refuel ourselves, in the form of a milkshake and a hamburger, at what was really a one-horse town. The milkshake was solid enough to eat with a knife and fork, but the hamburger was good. Just as light was fading, we passed the historic little town of Fort Benson, the second oldest settlement in Montana and, in 1961, it was awarded the title of being a national historic landmark. We arrived at our destination by 10.00pm, and after a good meal we got rooms in the Park Hotel, where we spent a comfortable night.

In the morning, after an English breakfast, we spent half an hour trying to find the road out of town and by the time we reached the highway it felt as if half the morning had passed. Of course, today's drivers just need a mobile phone with them which they can plug in and receive clear and polite directions from a computer voice. There were no such facilities in 1956 and so navigating was a tough job, even with maps.

The morning drive took us across ranch land and through the Missouri River canyon, which was awesome. The fast-flowing river had cut a deep gorge through the mountains and we stopped often to read the roadside notice boards giving historical information. We discovered we were following the tracks of the Lewis and Clark Expedition of 1805, a US military expedition to explore the Pacific Northwest, and we certainly felt intrepid and full of awe for those early pioneers who travelled these parts on horseback. We went through Helena, the capital of Montana, but did not stop. We continued to Butte, which is the centre of an important mining district. On the outskirts of the town, one of the roadside signs declared, 'The Richest Hill in the World'. This hill is almost entirely composed of an extremely rich copper ore. After a brief visit to the vast open cast mine, we had a late lunch in the Finlen Hotel. In the afternoon we crossed the Pipestone Pass, which has an elevation of 6,418 ft; the car took it without any difficulty, which was very encouraging.

The scenery was glorious and the road cut into the sides of cliffs which rose up almost vertically on either side. After crossing the mountains, we descended into the Jefferson Valley, named after Captain Jefferson who led an expedition in this district. Our road took us along the Jefferson River, which was the centre of the gold rush of the 1860s. One could still see the heaps of gravel which a hundred years previously had been sifted by the gold seekers. The highlight of our trip back in time came when we visited Virginia City. This tiny gold rush town had been preserved exactly as it was a century previously. We spent an hour or two examining the old shops, the forge and the saloon, which was complete with its original furnishings and music machines. Between Virginia City and the Yellowstone National Park was just open ranch land, so we elected to drive straight to West Yellowstone. As we set off in early evening, the roads were almost deserted as we had noted that Americans did not drive very much at night. We arrived at West Yellowstone at 10.30pm and hired a real log cabin for the night. Our total mileage since leaving Moose Jaw was 950 miles: the date was Sunday 19 August. All the American people we had met so far seemed very friendly and, as a general rule, they were more cheerful than Canadians. This was especially noticeable in shops, cafes and motels where we were greeted with 'service with a smile' almost always. America also felt much more developed than Canada, by which I mean better infrastructures and facilities and altogether a higher standard of living. Perhaps this is why they were more cheerful. But it was a feeling that all four of us shared after our trip.

We knew Yellowstone National Park would be one of the highlights of our holiday, so we got up early and allowed a whole day for our visit. This proved to be really quite inadequate but it was all the time we could afford. And we had had to buy another tyre for the car, after which we set out.

The park is very large and is almost completely covered by fir forests. Its elevation averages 7,000 ft, with several passes rising to 8,000 ft. The roads follow the rivers and lake shores most of the time, and provided wonderful vistas of waterfalls, hot springs and mud pools. After entering the park via the west entrance, we went to Madison Junction and then up the Gibbon River valley. We saw the Gibbon Falls which, although relatively small, are very pretty.

In addition to the beautiful scenery in the park, we encountered all kinds of wildlife too. There were literally hundreds of little chipmunks who would line the roadside, having learnt how to beg for food from tourists. Then there were the infamous bears which were very numerous in the park. Many times we had to bring the car to a rapid stop as a couple of bears had sauntered into the road and made their way up to the car looking for food. One even had the confidence to put its head into the car!

The first hot spring we came to was Beryl Spring which, with a temperature just below boiling point, is the hottest spring in the park. It has a beautiful colour but also a rather strong smell of sulphur. We continued on to the Yellowstone Grand Canyon 20 miles further along the road. On arriving, there was little to see until one left the car and walked to the edge of the canyon. What I then saw I shall never forget. Near vertical cliffs with a river 1,000 ft below and the colouring of every shade of red and brown combined to make a wonderful spectacle. It was difficult to drag ourselves away from the canyon and it was only the knowledge that there was still more to see that made it possible. We headed onward towards the Yellowstone Lake, which is the largest body of water at such an altitude in the USA. It covers an area of 139 square miles at an elevation of 7,731 ft above sea level. We motored along its shore for 20 miles and then went across Craig Pass to Old Faithful Geyser. This pass is 8,262 ft above sea level and crosses the Continental Divide, the principal, largely mountainous hydrological divide of the continent. It separates the watersheds that drain into the Pacific Ocean from those river systems that drain into the Atlantic or Arctic Oceans. We were lucky in that we arrived at Old Faithful about ten minutes before 'she' was due to erupt. Actually, I say lucky because on arrival Brian and I had rather foolishly had a quick peep into the geyser's 'mouth' which, if we had got our timing wrong, would have brought us to a very sudden demise. The more I think about Old Faithful, the more amazed I am by the phenomenon. Every hour, usually within a few minutes, a vast quantity of hot water is thrown 150 ft into the air. It's incredible. A park official gave a talk on the history of the geyser and how it works while we waited expectantly for its next eruption. We were not disappointed: the eruption itself lasted about two minutes and as the sun was shining, we saw it under ideal conditions. We had a rather late lunch in a restaurant at the geyser and saw another performance before leaving.

We had to retrace our tracks over Craig Pass and then headed south to continue our tour. After leaving the park our road took us close to the Teton Mountains which were still capped by snow, even though it was the height of summer. As the highest peak is 13,766 ft above sea level, it is little surprise that the snow remains throughout the year. By now it was getting quite late in the evening but we wanted to get within striking distance of Salt Lake City for the night so we would cross the Bonneville Salt Flats before dark next day. We therefore drove on across the Wyoming ranch land until 10.00pm, when we put up in a small town called Kemmerer. Our total mileage now stood at 1,200 miles and the day was Monday. So far the weather had been very pleasant with temperatures around the 80 degree mark.

Tuesday 20 August dawned and we headed towards Salt Lake City. The car was running well and we made it by lunchtime. After a little shopping and lunch, we set off for a swim in the lake. The water in the lake contains about 27 per cent salt and therefore it is literally impossible to sink in it. It is also nearly impossible to swim normally, as one's feet just splash around on the surface which makes for an uncanny sensation but very enjoyable nonetheless. Having made sure that we had an adequate supply of gas, oil and water, we set off across the Great Salt Lake Desert. For 100 miles all we saw was dirty looking sand and small dry shrubs. The last 10 miles were across the Bonneville Salt Flats where the land speed records have been set. This vast expanse of glistening white salt is perfectly flat for an area 20 miles long and 5 miles wide. There is absolutely nothing in the way of life or vegetation. The road and railway run dead straight for 20 miles and the curvature of the

Earth is plainly visible when looking along the telegraph poles. Mirages are very common. We reached the town of Wendover on the western edge of the desert, which was first built solely as a railway town but was now quite a large place, but we motored on for another 100 miles that evening and spent the night at Elko.

The next day's drive was across the Nevada Desert and the scenery was unchanged; dry sandy soil covered by shrubs with small ranges of hills occasionally breaking the monotony. We found a very nice motel on the outskirts of Reno and booked in for the night. In Nevada, in fact throughout the USA, as in Canada, one must be twenty-one years of age to be allowed to gamble or to drink alcohol. The first setback came when we were not even allowed to enter a restaurant where liquor was being sold! But we felt we really could not leave Reno without at least a few pulls on the one arm bandits: we were tourists in the truest sense of the word and wanted to experience everything that our tour could offer. In Reno this was gambling. Once more, our dear friend John came to the rescue and he obtained the necessary tickets for us all to get in and try our luck. Before long, our ruse was discovered and we were lucky to get away with only threats to call the police. I still find it odd that America is so conservative (with a small c) in these laws but is happy to let people who are younger walk around with guns. We walked around the city, found a pleasant restaurant to eat and decided to go to the cinema. The movie did not finish until 1.30am.

We left Reno none too early the following day and set out for the city by the Golden Gate Bridge. Soon after leaving, we made a small excursion to Lake Tahoe, which is reputed to be one of the most beautiful lakes in the USA. Did it live up to its reputation? It certainly did: an expanse of clear, cobalt-blue water, tucked into the snowy Sierra Nevada mountain range and the second deepest lake in the whole of the US. We enjoyed a quick brunch on the lake's shores but did not have time to spare. Back on the road, we went over the Donner Pass which has an elevation of over 7,000 ft. The road climbs steeply up the side of a mountain and the view looking back was particularly beautiful. The car was still running well, although the clutch was starting to give trouble again. The road through the mountains was very 'English' in character, by which I mean it was narrow and full of twists and turns, but as we approached Sacramento, we came upon a vast eight-lane highway and the miles soon slipped by. However, by sheer bad luck we found ourselves caught up in the Sacramento rush hour, which did not help the Dodge's clutch. The road to San Francisco was super highways all the way and we all had to pay attention to ensure we got in the right lanes, but eventually we found ourselves on the San Francisco–Oakland Bay Bridge: the famous Golden Gate Bridge. This bridge is 8¼ miles long, consisting of two sections with an island in the middle. At this time of day, the traffic was quite fantastic, as every lane was full but with the whole lot motoring at 60 mph.

San Francisco was such a large city compared to anything we had been to before that we seemed to go twice round it before getting our bearings. Eventually we found the motels and we got rooms in one on the outskirts of the city. As we switched off the engine the mileage was 2,150. In the evening we went into the city and had a very pleasant meal at a restaurant serving a 'ranch house' style dinner. This is a system whereby one pays a fixed price for a ticket and is then allowed to eat as much as one wants. The invitation was just too tempting to four young men as we piled delicious food on to our out-sized plates. We turned in early but were still rather late rising.

We were keen to visit San Francisco's Chinatown. It is entirely populated by Chinese people, the shops sell genuine Chinese goods and even the smells are authentic and makes the atmosphere really complete. After buying a few souvenirs and taking some photographs, we climbed the steep hill to the famous Mark Hopkins Hotel. The view from the 'Top of the Mark' is one a tourist must not miss, so we duly took the elevator all the way up and enjoyed the wonderful view of the city and both its famous bridges. In the evening we decided to go to a nightclub and after consulting all the guidebooks we chose 'Charlie Lowe's Forbidden City' for another authentic Chinese experience. We had a very fine meal and saw the Chinese floor show which included some wonderful acrobats. Eventually, at some early hour in the morning we made our way back to the Mission Bell Hotel.

After two days of touring San Francisco and its hills, the clutch on our car was completely burnt out and it was obvious that we would have to do something about it before we left. On the Saturday morning we decided to take a look around the second-hand car dealers with the idea of buying another car. We were delighted to discover that for $300 we could get a very reasonable car, so we traded the old Dodge for a 1950 Nash Statesman Super!

After an enormous pile of paperwork had been completed, John A. Robbins was the proud, registered owner and we drove off in our new steed. The deal cost each of us $67 – plus the Dodge as a trade-in.

In the afternoon we went to see the Barbary Coast, which was a notorious place in the days of the sailing ships. Here we saw the British barque *Baraclutha*, a 'round the Cape' vessel which had been kept just as she was when in service from approximately 1860 to 1890 when steam power took over. After taking a look round her, we set off to see the Golden Gate Bridge. None of us had imagined it to be so large; I think this must be because it is so perfectly proportioned. We decided to save the experience of driving over it until we left the city, but we spent a good amount of time admiring it.

When we finally tore ourselves from the view, we drove off and it quickly became apparent that all was not well with the new car. Every time we stepped on the accelerator, it misfired, and badly. We four, each having a degree of knowledge about engines, suspected carburettor trouble so we stopped at a garage where we unsuccessfully tried to cure the trouble. But then followed just about the worst car journey imaginable. The engine refused to idle and every time we tried to accelerate the engine cut violently. To make matters worse we hit San Francisco's rush hour. It took us over two hours to cross the city and we left a trail of chaos in our wake! That evening we really cursed the Nash but come the morning, with fresh eyes and fresh heads, we chanced to discover that the ignition coil, which was mounted on the engine, was loose and was making an intermittent contact. Problem fixed! To celebrate we headed to the Pacific coast where we had lunch and a bathe in the sea. Contrary to popular belief, the Pacific Ocean is not gloriously warm (at least not at San Francisco), but we had a wonderful bathe all the same. That evening we went to the cinema where we saw *The King and I*, which was quite the best musical any of us had seen.

The next morning it was time to leave San Francisco and we drove out across the Golden Gate Bridge which, somewhat disappointingly, was partially hidden by low clouds. We had been wise to take in the view of it when we had had the opportunity, as it seems that, given the micro-climate in the Bay area, it is an often occurrence for it to be hidden by low cloud. The roads were very good and the miles slipped by very quickly as the car was running well. Our journey took us past the famous Redwood forests which are known the world over for their giant, ancient trees and beautiful scenery. We stopped quite often and enjoyed delights such as the 'One Log House' (which is about the size of a caravan); a beautiful tree house and a tree so large that careful drivers can drive a car through a hole in its trunk. This was a challenge not to be missed, but it was a tight fit for our wide Nash. We made it with only a scratch. On the first day out of San Francisco we got as far as Crescent City about 400 miles up the coast, where we checked into a motel for the night.

The next day was Tuesday and we set out fairly early so we would have plenty of time at Crater Lake, which would be the point of interest in the day's run. The Crater Lake National Park is about 200 miles from Crescent City and we arrived there in the middle of the afternoon. There is a stiff climb on the road to the summit of the lake rim, which is about 8,000 ft above sea level, and when we arrived it afforded us a glorious view of the lake under what can only be described as ideal conditions: a clear blue sky with the sun glistening on the water. It really deserves all that is said about it for it was certainly one of the most beautiful sights that any of us had ever seen. The water was perfectly still and a deep royal blue colour. It is believed to be 2,000 ft deep, which would explain the intensity and richness of the colour. The cliffs surrounding the lake rise 100 ft above it and are of all different colours. We spent an hour or two there and then motored on to a very pleasant cafe where we had a meal before going on to Rhododendron to spend the night in an exceptionally plush motel. We had a large living room, a kitchen, bathroom and two double bedrooms – all for $10. We felt like kings.

The next day's journey took us through Portland, Tacoma and Seattle, which are all very busy American cities and the traffic was heavy all day. When we passed through Seattle, we saw the Boeing factory which was producing B52 bombers at a fantastic rate. The area around the factory building is packed tight with aircraft under construction, all lined up along the factory's perimeters, so we were able to get a good look at them as we passed. Once again our bad luck meant we hit rush hour and found ourselves amongst thousands of Boeing workers all trying to get their cars on to the already packed road, but I suppose it afforded us more time to look at the aircraft.

When we got to the customs at the border, we discovered that by selling

En route through
California.

The drive-through tree.

Author buried alive
in California.

a Canadian car in the USA we had broken almost every rule in the book of regulations. We were mortified but thankfully we met with a very nice American official who just laughed at us and reasoned that the car probably was not worth any bother anyway. The Canadian customs officers were a little more formal and had to look up the special regulations for NATO personnel before deciding that they could allow the Nash into the country. So it was with a rather large sigh of relief when we finally drove back across into Canada, and none the poorer. As it was now after dark, we stopped at the first hotel we found with rooms available. It was not the best night's sleep for any of us.

The following morning, we gladly left the terrible hotel and drove over the Lion's Gate Bridge to north Vancouver where we had breakfast whilst we watched the city wake and bustle into action. Whilst doing this, we met the Belgian boys we helped at the beginning of the leave. They had hitch-hiked as far as Los Angeles and were now on their way back to Moose Jaw with a Canadian from our course.

We had made a visit to the Tourist Information Office to find out what Vancouver had to offer and after lunch we went for a drive along the shoreline and had a round of miniature golf. This proved to be very entertaining, since I was the only one who had ever played the game before. We continued with a visit to the totem pole at Prospect Point, from where we had a fine view of the Lion Gate Bridge and the entrance to Vancouver Harbour. We decided to take a ride up the Grouse Mountain chairlift and this, for me, was one of the most pleasant parts of the holiday. We went up in the late afternoon and enjoyed a wonderful view of the city below. This time of day is best for viewing the city, as in the morning there is usually a heavy mist in the valley. At the summit, which is 3,000 ft high, we enjoyed some light refreshments before the descent. By now it was almost dark and we watched as the lights came on in the city below, twinkling in the bluey hue of twilight.

The next day, a Friday, we set out fairly early and stopped at a service station where we had breakfast and got the car greased in preparation for the roads ahead. We had enjoyed some wonderful motoring and good roads but we knew we were heading for mountain country where the conditions might not be so favourable. The roads were in fact good most of the way until we left the trunk road and headed north across the Rockies where they became rough owing to construction work. The scenery was very impressive and consisted mainly of coniferous forests on the sides of enormous mountains. At Kelowna we took the ferry and crossed the Okanagan Lake and then continued to Vernon. It was now dark and soon the road deteriorated to a gravel track with numerous hazardous detours. All this section was being reconstructed and would eventually be part of the Trans-Canada Highway. After a very tiring drive late into the evening we stopped at Revelstoke which is a small town in the midst of a tremendous mountain range. The motel only had three beds available and so Brian drew the short straw and slept in the car. He nearly froze to death! The temperature plummets at night-time in the mountain areas.

Before continuing our journey, we took the car to a service station to see if we could cure a bumping noise that had developed. We were dismayed to discover that the rear engine mountings were broken and there was little we could do there except hope the engine would not drop out before we reached Moose Jaw! The owner of the service station was an ex-RAF officer who had flown bombers in the war. By some bizarre coincidence, he had also been a swimming instructor at Tony's old school! The world is a very small place indeed.

It was a Saturday and we knew we had 193 miles of rough road ahead before we would reach a town called Golden, so called as some miners had indeed struck gold there. The road from Revelstoke to Golden was called 'Big Bend' and a glance at the map shows why. I could not help but notice that Canadians and Americans like to keep their place names simple. Along this stretch of road, which was only really gravel, there were only about three inhabited settlements and the road surface was terrible, really terrible. The redeeming feature was the scenery, which was simply glorious, and of course the reason why we chose this particular route. The car stood up to the drive very well in spite of its troubles and we reached Golden by teatime. However, our journeying over rough roads was not yet finished as the road east of Golden was also 'under construction'! Always the Canadian roads were 'under construction'. However, at last we came to a surfaced road and had a very pleasant drive through the last of the Rocky Mountains. As the sun was setting we drove over Kicking Horse Pass, once more crossing the Continental Divide. We arrived in Banff shortly after and put up in a hotel in what appeared to be the last two vacant rooms in Banff. It was a holiday weekend and it seemed as though everyone within 500 miles, including many cadets from Moose Jaw, had come to Banff for the holiday.

After a well-earned rest we dragged ourselves out of bed only to find the weather was anything but pleasant and not at all suitable for enjoying the Banff scenery. It was cold and cloudy, but we put on all our sweaters and went for a drive up the mountain to the chairlift. When we arrived there, it actually started to snow, so we decided not to take a ride further into the cloud and snow.

The car was giving some trouble in selecting gears, as the gear box kept moving, so we drove to a service station where we administered some automobile First Aid. It was a proper triage job – we just had to get the car back to Moose Jaw and so we fixed the problem by raising the rear end of the engine with a block of wood! As the weather continued to be cold and rather dismal, we decided to push on and set out eastwards. It was not long before we had left the mountains for good, stopping only at Calgary for lunch. We drove fast all day and arrived at Swift Current in the evening. This left us with only 100 miles to drive the following day. For the first time on the holiday, we took four single rooms instead of two doubles and slept soundly as a result.

We arrived back in Saskatchewan with a gale blowing to welcome us. It seemed very dull after all the wonderful country we had visited and the amazing experiences we had had. On arrival in Moose Jaw, we had motored an incredible 4,988 miles. We had not had a single accident nor any really serious trouble with either car. All together it had been a very successful holiday, extremely enjoyable and enlightening.

Sixty-five years later, as I reflect on this wonderful adventure, I can still vividly remember so much of it. I remember the awesome scale and majesty of the landscape of western USA and Canada; so different when viewed from a car or on foot, rather than from the air. I remember, too, the warm and friendly hospitality of the American and Canadian people we met on the way, and I also remember that there was never a cross word between us four friends. Remarkable really. The shared experience would cement our friendship for life, and I am deeply indebted to each of them for such rich and rewarding companionship. I am particularly grateful to my dear friend Brian Stevens for his copious notes and comments on our unique trip, which I have used extensively in writing this chapter.

CHAPTER EIGHT
REAL FLYING TOWARDS WINGS

WITH THE SUMMER vacation over we returned to the serious business of flying and training. We had already completed the relatively easy bit of learning how to take off, fly and land a Harvard safely: the bare bones so to speak. Up next would be navigation skills, night flying, instrument flying and aerobatics, which may seem like the fun part, but the reasoning behind it was much more serious: to out-manoeuvre an enemy. Finally, we would be taught the disciplines of formation flying. The word 'discipline' was on my mind, as I knew all of us on course 5517 would be starting this second stage of training with a session with the officer in charge of training along with our own instructor for feedback on our progress so far. On the second day back on base, I was called in for my feedback. The message was this:

> Morris, you have the potential to be a very good pilot. You think quickly, are careful and have sensitive fingers. Your instrument flying is exceptional, indeed one of the top three. However, there are two serious weaknesses. Firstly, you do not move your head around anywhere near enough. If you were in a dog fight you would miss seeing half the enemy. Add to this, your aerobatics are only average. We have decided you need a new instructor who will be tougher on you and this will be Flying Officer Filo. You will fly with him this afternoon.

Indeed, I did, and I logged 1 hour 10 minutes' dual flying time, followed by a whole hour with my instructor to analyse it. Filo was a man of few words, and these were far outnumbered by his liberal use of expletives – quite possibly more than I had ever heard before. However, his teaching was informed and inspired, and I took it all in as I was determined to succeed.

There followed three months of intensive flying with navigational trips each lasting two hours. Many more hours were spent in the planning of these trips, which took a great deal of care and attention. Nobody wanted the shame of getting lost whilst out on a flight and, being the prairies, there was a lot of very flat land with few distinguishing landmarks. However, as a very last resort, there was the option to fly low and read the wording on the side of a grain silo to understand where one was. I confess I did it once, just to reassure myself, but there were some colleagues who had greater difficulty with their navigation and came to rely on those silos!

I particularly enjoyed the night flying and our one navigation sortie. However, one colleague somehow lost his way in the dark and drifted over the US border which was barely five minutes' flying time due south from Moose Jaw. Perhaps he was one who had come to rely on the silos as his navigational aid which, cloaked under the cover of darkness, could no longer help him. No sooner was he over the border than two Sabre jets were either side of him and forced him to land. He was held for a day, one I am sure he will never forget, before flying back and led straight into the Commanding Officer's office for a sharp dressing down. A diplomatic disaster narrowly avoided. However, there were more light-hearted moments, such as the report from a colleague about one navigational flight where he noticed the chap ahead of him kept flying at regular intervals inverted. This was a navigational flight, not an aerobatics exercise. Our colleague quizzed the man in front and the answer came back loud and clear: 'I'm trying to pick up my banana which fell on the cockpit floor.' As the days passed, my own aerobatics did improve but I was outclassed by others on the course, including Neil Williams who later became aerobatic world champion. I seem to remember my roommate Brian Stevens was pretty good too.

I improved with time and my instructor, Flying Officer Filo, mellowed. On a bright day in early October, he told me that the day's lesson would be practising low flying around the river and lakes. I cannot remember exactly how low we were, but it was very low, and we took in several of the smaller lakes and even some large ponds on our trip. We repeated this exercise for several Fridays in a row: we visited a vast number of nearby patches of water and sometimes we flew over the same one again and again. Eventually, I plucked up courage and asked him why and what the point of the exercise was. His reply was characteristically forthright: 'The answer is simple: whilst you are improving your low flying skills (and you are doing well), I am spotting the location of the wild ducks for the next day's shoot!' A couple of years ago, I suggested to colleagues in my local shoot in Sandy, Bedfordshire that we might try the same with an aircraft out of Shuttleworth but the gamekeeper was horrified.

I could not wait to learn how to fly in formation and at last, on 29 October, Filo announced that we were to start. We were to begin with a two-plane formation and would build up to four planes. Then two weeks later, on 14 November, as we put on our parachutes, we were greeted with the exciting news that we would have 1 hour 45 minutes of flying time in formation. Flying Officer Filo expertly led the flying whilst simultaneously providing a running commentary of directions so that we all moved from one position to another. I felt elated.

On 16 November, just two days later, I took off and joined three other colleagues in our own four-plane formation. This time there was no Flying Officer Filo, or any other instructor, to give the directions. We were on our own and knew we were being observed. We each took turns to be the lead aircraft and flew in every position. It was simply wonderful, and I think we all felt that we had truly begun to master the skies. On landing we had a formal de-briefing which was encouragingly positive and was just as well as we were approaching the end of the course at Moose Jaw.

On 27 November, two days after my twentieth birthday, my instructor and I joined a four-plane formation for a 1 hour 30 minute flight. This was followed by my own personal four-plane test, which also lasted 1 hour 30 minutes, and which I passed with flying colours. Joy of joys, I was told I could then join my original four-plane formation for our final flight at Moose Jaw. We made our plans and sought permission for a fly-past, with dipped wings, of the control tower before we broke off to land. Someone suggested a victory roll but that was vetoed, but still, it was quite possibly one of the best birthday presents I could have wished for.

It was also something of a bittersweet moment, as we had now been stationed at Moose Jaw for eight months and our time there was coming to an end. It was a time for reflection on what we had learnt and experienced, not just in the aircraft and the four walls of the classroom, but of Saskatchewan and its people; a province, and a nation new to us all.

I think all of us had been into Moose Jaw itself a few times, but it was not the most exciting place for young men in search of fun and entertainment. I feel sure that our earliest experiences of trying to meet with local girls was representative of how many of the locals felt about us: 'Beware Pilots from the Air Force.' I had made an effort and sampled the local tennis club but found neither the quality of play nor the company particularly appealing, so I took it no further. In contrast, we did enjoy going to the drive-in cinema in our dear old Dodge. That was something that we had never experienced in England. Indeed, I remember at one drive-in, Brian (Ginger) was caught climbing out of the boot trying to avoid buying a ticket. Net result? We were thrown out!

Ginger was probably the most experienced car driver of the four of us, but he always seemed to attract challenges. I remember one such example with him at the wheel and the rest of us dozing, when a large red light attached to a police car appeared beside the Dodge and started flashing a stop sign at us. Ginger woke us all with shouts of, 'What shall I do?' After receiving hours of careful direction from our flying instructors, we decided to adopt a similar approach. We told him to slow down, pull over, lower the window and politely explain to the officer that we were British flying cadets from Moose Jaw. Ginger did as we instructed, with all the charm and grace he could muster and, thankfully, we were waved on our way.

As to meeting members of the opposite sex, it seemed incredibly difficult. To the best of my memory only David Cobbold met up with and had a friendship that lasted beyond our period in Canada. However, there was one initiative that we four thought we would take which, looking back now, shows just how keen we were for some female company. We each agreed that the local telephone operator had a really seductive and inviting voice, and based on this alone we reasoned that we would all like to meet her. We discussed, at length, how we could make this a reality and decided that we could visit her at the telephone exchange. Putting all our heads together, we researched and found out where it was and how to get into it. It was not easy! We then drew lots and I got the black spot. Armed with a story we had jointly concocted to explain why I would be visiting the telephone exchange, I set off full of the confidence of youth. On arrival, I knocked on the door and awaited the response. The door opened and there stood the object of our desires, asking how she might help me. She was not the beautiful siren we had all imagined, but instead, the plainest lady of middle age that I had ever met. Mission most definitely not successful.

However, what was more successful was my relationship with my girlfriend Ann. I would write to her twice a week, every week, telling her all my news and stories. She would write back twice a week on airmail 'blue-ies', always signing off with a kiss in red lipstick; really romantic. Sadly, the letters we sent each other were thrown away when we departed to work in India in 1961, but in 2021, at the time of writing this, we celebrated our 61st wedding anniversary.

It was unanimously agreed that course 5517 had been a success. We had enjoyed ourselves and each had learnt a huge amount. However, almost at the last minute, we realised we did not have a course badge. I did some local research, found someone to make it for us and volunteered to sketch out a few designs. David Cobbold agreed to think of an appropriate motto. The final design showed a rising phoenix with the motto 'Cogito Ergo Sum' (Descartes) which in English translates to 'I think therefore I am'. As a pilot, if one does not think, one crashes and is killed, and therefore is no longer. The badge was adopted by all on the course and a copy of it was fixed on the wall of the bar. My copy is framed and has pride of place in my study alongside my RAF Wings.

As I reflected on my time at Moose Jaw and researched this chapter, I read in the July–September 2021 issue of *Air Mail*, the RAF Association's quarterly magazine for its members, that HRH the Duke of Edinburgh had also flown a Harvard during his flying training. Apparently, he had to complete three solo circuits and landings at White Waltham airfield to qualify for his wings. An examining unit had described his flying as 'thoughtful with a sense of safety and airmanship above average' (source: MOD/Crown 1953). Well, the late Duke certainly had some very special talents.

My own record of flying Harvards at Moose Jaw involved considerably more flying hours than those of the Duke. Over five months, I completed 171 flights totalling 78 hours' solo and 108 hours' dual flying time. What a magical experience it was. I flew in skies of brilliant, bright sunshine reflected off white snow below, in skies with no cloud cover at all and in cumulus nimbus clouds which could appear out of nowhere and would require every plane to return to base immediately. No one could ask for a more varied, exciting time, and it will remain etched in my memory forever.

T33 – formation flying.
(William March)

Our Course 5517 at
RCAF MacDonald.

John ready to fly.

CHAPTER NINE
RCAF MACDONALD JET WINGS

OUR JOURNEY IN the Nash from RCAF Moose Jaw to RCAF MacDonald took place in the middle of winter with temperatures in the -20s. It was a good straight road but engineered for vehicle speeds of around 40 mph. Snow blowers had been out and the snow was piled up on the embankments either side of the road. We passed two at work, which was a sight none of us had seen before and made us wonder why we did not have any in the UK, such was their efficiency. However, this was in the days when winters were really cold, both in England and in northern America, not like today. We followed our well-practised technique for changing drivers, so no time was lost and we made good time. We drove into RCAF MacDonald in the evening and were delighted with the organisation of our sleeping quarters and overall friendliness, finding warmth in our first meal and relaxation in the Mess bar. The date was 8 December and although we did not know at the time, the only jet flying we would do before Christmas would be a familiarising flight with our instructor.

Next morning the Wing Commander in charge of OC Flying No 4 Advanced Flying School (SE) welcomed us with a rousing speech that really got us fired up:

> Gentlemen.... Welcome to the Jet age and in particular to the T33 Canadair Silver Star. This is the most modern jet trainer in the world with a ceiling of 47,000 ft which is just under 9 miles from Earth. As one of my predecessors said, you are going to be fighter pilots and every man a tiger!

We had presumed we would begin our ground instructions with a series of lectures on the mechanics of the T33 aircraft, but we were very much mistaken. The Wing Commander wasted no time and got straight on with the very important business of parachute training. If we had been in any doubt before this first lecture about the potential danger of what we were doing, it was quickly dispelled as the Wing Commander continued. He stated with absolute clarity that every pilot must be fully conversant with how the parachutes worked, and as an indication of how important they were, he himself would be delivering the lecture. Moreover, he reminded us that it was part of the UK's Queen's Regulations and Air Ministry of Canada Instruction which decreed that all aircrew in the air forces of the UK and overseas dominions must be equipped with a parachute and that Canada supported this whole-heartedly. In essence, the drill itself was very simple and we were all to be issued with a back-type parachute rather like a haversack. The purpose of the lecture, however, was slightly more complex, as it focused on survival techniques to be used in the event of a pilot having to evacuate/eject from an aircraft. The Wing Commander explained that the T33 was one of the world's safest jets, with next to no vices. However, we would be training above some of the world's most inhospitable terrain, and he reminded us that our country had invested a great deal of time and money in training us thus far. If there was an accident, the RCAF would be responsible and therefore wanted to give us the best chances of survival.

Key point number 1: familiarise yourself with the oxygen bottle attached to the parachute harness. Its purpose is to keep a pilot alive if he has to eject at high altitude.

Key point number 2: unplug your radio lead and plug in the oxygen lead into the bottle before hitting the eject button. The canopy blasts off first and then you follow it and disappear off into the atmosphere, together with your seat. You must then undo your straps and kick yourself clear of the seat, quickly and calmly.

Key point number 3: get your parachute ready. You may well be at 40,000 ft where the temperature may be as much as 100 degrees below freezing. The temptation will be to pull the rip cord too soon but you must wait for three long minutes of free fall. Time it on your watch. If you do not, you will be frozen to death and come down to earth as an iceberg!

Nobody dared to ask how many times anyone had had to eject.

We were then shown all the equipment, including a specially created seat cushion, designed by the Canadians, which we were advised had to be clicked on to the parachute harness immediately on entering the cockpit. 'The cushion attached to your "butt" can possibly save your life.' The use of the slang word 'butt' by a man of such standing, certainly made us sit up and pay attention. He was very straight talking. I decided to be bold and asked the question that everyone was thinking: what was in the cushion that ensured it would save our life? The Commander proceeded to point out a zip which ran along the length of it. With a great sense of showmanship, he unzipped it with a flourish and revealed an all-metal Hornet .22 rifle. This was to be used to kill animals to provide us with food. There was also a small mirror with a hole in the middle and a sighting loop attached, for flashing reflected sunlight to attract any high-flying aircraft; fishing gear, matches, survival rations, spare socks, compass, a first aid kit, food tins, survival booklet, knife, water-bladder, gloves and a blanket, all packed neatly into the cushion. It was quite remarkable. We were told we would be shown a training film with a demonstration of how to use everything: assuming we could shoot straight with the .22 to kill a rabbit!

We would continue in the weeks before Christmas with a number of ground training exercises, including meteorology, navigation and engineering, which had to be completed before we could even think of going airborne. We would have a familiarising flight soon after Christmas, but real flying and teaching would only start in mid-January when everyone was back from leave. However, the rising tension in the Middle East, particularly over the Suez Canal, had persuaded the authorities that our course should push ahead with all possible speed and should aim to be completed by Easter, which was at the beginning of April; in effect, just three months away. I do not think any of us were worried by this expectation. By this time, we had been in Canada long enough to have completed a good number of hours of flying and indeed long enough even to have gained a twang in our voices. We were itching to earn our Wings and above all to have intensive, full-on teaching from the world's best trainers. We were excited to start after the Christmas break.

Christmas 1956: I received a call from my mother inviting me and my three nearest and dearest friends to join her and my father in Ottawa for

Christmas. By a bizarre twist of fate, my father had been appointed to a senior position as a city architect there. The challenge was how we would get there, as it was some 1,300 miles from RCAF MacDonald. The four of us chatted to our Canadian friends and instructors and asked their advice. Simple, said one: 'Get hold of Winnipeg, explain you are four Brits on this course and is there any chance of hitching a lift on any transport going to Ottawa.' He made it sound as easy as calling for a taxi-cab. Nevertheless, we tried it and much to our astonishment we discovered that there was indeed a plane going from Winnipeg to Ottawa. We accepted the offer, leapt into the car and drove to Winnipeg in time for the flight departure on 18 December. Tony says it was a RCAF North Star, I think it was a Mitchell bomber, but that doesn't matter, we were just all so excited to be having an English Christmas. I have to say, such was the excitement that we did not give a second thought to the return journey at the time, but that was for later. My parents put on a good show and we all enjoyed a wonderful time together. My brothers were both there, too, so it really was a proper family reunion and my mother even managed to continue the family tradition of putting silver thruppence pieces in the Christmas pudding, one for each of us brothers to find.

We had to be back on base by 27 December, but we had been told that no one would fly on the 25th or 26th. However, fortune favours the brave, and in this case the young and impulsive, and we were lucky to receive a call on the 22nd advising us that a Dakota was going to Winnipeg on 26th. It would be virtually empty and there would be plenty of room for us. This was just as well as I was to have my familiarising flight on 27 December with my new instructor Flying Officer Campbell.

I was ready in good time and prepared with my new silk scarf to protect my neck with all the necessary turning of my head. There were two flying helmets: one of canvass with the earphones embedded in it and the other which fitted over the top; a sort of large white crash helmet, lovingly called 'the bone dome'. In addition, there was a large green oxygen mask covering nearly all of one's face. Once fully kitted out you cannot hear anything from the outside so one only puts them on when ready to climb into the jet.

Flying Officer Campbell explained what we were going to do, and I immediately felt a rapport with him. I listened intently as this would be my first ever flight in a former US frontline fighter jet from the Korean War, then known as the Lockheed P-80 Shooting Star. Campbell took time to remind me of the differences from the dear Harvard. There was no propeller, no torque, no vibration, but instead a huge acceleration created by 2½ tons of thrust and more than 600 gallons of juice which would not only launch the aircraft but could keep it airborne for at least three hours (although my first flight would only be for thirty minutes). He added, with what I believe was a great sense of pride, the engine was now the Rolls-Royce Nene which made it an even better plane with a 1,000 lbs more thrust than the USAF Allison-powered aircraft. In my research I discovered that Rolls-Royce even managed to sell the Nene engine to the Russians for their MiGs. Given this early triumph, I do wonder if over the years UK governments have given Rolls-Royce enough help and support.

We walked across a snow-covered path, carrying our parachutes to do the external, pre-pre-flight, take-off checks. I did not know the exact temperature, but it was really cold and reassured me that Manitoba deserved its title of being the coldest province in Canada. We put on both our helmets, our backpack parachutes and then climbed aboard using the hook-on ladder. Some days it was too cold to walk outside, so we climbed into the aircraft in the hangar and were then towed out to the parking area.

Campbell took great care to run through the 'abandon aircraft procedure', pointing out the canopy ejection lever and also making sure my oxygen pipe was properly in its socket. I remembered the Wing Commander's opening lecture and how right he had been to make it first business for us young pilots. Campbell settled into the rear cockpit; over our intercom he talked me through the starting procedure. The cockpit was pressurised as we taxied out to the runway. I was told to put my hands lightly on the controls. The order came 'Brakes on: Power on.' Then, 'Brakes off' to move slowly down the runway. Initially we moved slowly and then the speed leapt up and before I knew it, we were airborne. The wheels, a tricycle at the front, were stowed as we climbed effortlessly to 10,000 ft. Then, over the intercom came the words: 'You have control.' Training had taught me to respond in a heartbeat, with, 'I have control,' but there is still a split second in which to appreciate what that means and how it feels. For me, it was a feeling of complete elation. We continued to climb to 30,000 ft and I was pleased to hear Campbell's voice again: 'Well done, you are moving your head all the time.' At 30,000 ft we levelled off and as if giving voice to my own inner thoughts, Campbell said: 'Just look at the landscape beneath us; covered in snow but awe-inspiring beauty in this sunlight.' He was absolutely right; to me it seemed utterly magical.

But then the moment to admire the view had passed and Campbell advised me to 'Hold tight' as we were going to put the T33 through its paces. He added that he hoped I would not get airsick, and I fervently hoped so too. We embarked on aerobatics fit for a competition pulling G forces and, diving at 400 mph, we looped the loop. He offered some reassurance that if we got into any kind of trouble we could glide and land at another airbase, but that was only a precautionary measure, as he wanted to show me what the top speed felt like. As I looked down at the controls, I could see that the speed had been creeping up quite steadily but as the journey thus far had been so smooth, I had not realised just how fast we were travelling. Then, all of a sudden the aircraft began to shudder and shake and vibrate but, perhaps surprisingly, I did not feel nervous. We had all been briefed so thoroughly on the ground that I knew exactly what to expect. Then the intercom kicked in again and Campbell explained: 'If you go over Mach 0.8 she'll be in danger of breaking up! Remember too at 30,000 ft the speed of sound is a lot slower than at sea level.' We returned to Earth and landed T33 number 21142. I felt both exhilarated and yet exhausted from the adrenalin rush. Although I had experienced a huge range of emotions and sensations, airsickness had not been one of them. I was relieved.

I would not get to fly again for another two weeks. In a course of three months' duration, this felt like a very long time, and following my first flight with Campbell, I was charged and left desperately wanting more. However, the weather was poor with hailstones the size of pigeon's eggs, and patience is one of the most important skills for a pilot to learn. In addition, there was plenty of training to be done on the ground and it was all vital stuff: I had to go through a decompression experience/test which made one think of the challenge of flying using oxygen. We watched a training film about it, and it was frightening to see what happens to a man's body when the oxygen is switched off. We also had to experience the decompression chamber ourselves and learn the drills until we literally knew them by heart. There was also intensive training in a mock cockpit, with all the instruments which

T33 head on.

T33 instructor giving
instruction on the
ground.
(William March)

T33 formation with
author flying MH 172.
(Ginger, Brian Stevens)

A T33 diving down to Earth. (William March)

A T33 in beautiful profile. (William March)

Author's proudest day – the presentation of RAF Wings.

we used to familiarise ourselves with its layout so that we could almost come to rely on muscle memory during our drills and procedures. In addition, we received a weekly lecture on aviation medicine and on how to survive after parachuting or crash landing.

On 15 January, I was finally given permission to start flying again, with my instructor, and there followed four days of intensive flying with each flight lasting 1 hour 30 minutes. It was wonderful. Then, joy of joys, Flying Officer Campbell came to me and said:

Morris, this your special day. You are ready for solo. Go to your aircraft, number 21142, which you may remember is the first fighter jet you flew in with me. Now she is yours. Bring her back safely. You know what to do for the next 1 hour 15 minutes – Good luck.

Here was I, just twenty years of age, about to fly what was the best front-line fighter in the world of its day. Even Biggles would have been thrilled! I completed all my pre-flight checks and climbed on board. The flight went well and I managed to complete all manoeuvres I was told to do before returning to the ground. I thought the landing went well and was thrilled when my instructor said so too. Now I was on a roll: the next day we flew again for another 1 hour 20 minutes, which included some aerobatics followed by another solo trip in which I repeated the aerobatics.

The pressure was really on now, and in order to ensure we were all in peak physical fitness we embarked on special ARC exercises ('Addiction Recovery Coaching', so called as they were first employed on those recovering from additions to drugs and/or alcohol to build up the body. However, they were soon taken on by the military as part of their training, as the exercises proved to be so useful and beneficial). They are designed to build up the body's cells so the body can work harder and concentration powers are improved. Today's elite athletes use similar methods to improve their performances. We also worked with the Link trainer; a special bit of kit to enable pilots, on the ground, to better understand the nuances of instrument flying. The Link trainer was named after its creator and designer, Edwin Link, and it could simulate various conditions, including wind drift, turbulence and radio static. Our mornings were thus employed, followed by a test flight in the afternoon.

The flying and the training continued. Our abilities grew, as did our confidence. Then, with a mere three weeks of the course left to run, we finally started formation flying. My logbook tells me this was on 1 March and that I flew for over an hour. Initially, I linked up with one other aircraft and then with three others in what I think was called a 'finger left formation'.

Three days later, my dear late friend Pilot Officer Elsegood and I flew our respective T33s in a two-man formation across the skies for a total of 1 hour 30 minutes. It was a brilliant day for flying with gorgeous sunlight which, as we banked our aircraft, flashed off our silver wings.

The next day, the focus was on navigation and boy does one cover a lot of ground and fast in a jet. One really must concentrate, as there are not too many natural landmarks from which to get one's bearings in northern Manitoba.

By this point, we were flying five days a week, mission after mission, including night navigation and formation flying, and it was not long before we had clocked up a fantastic fifty-four missions. Even so, I found time to check out for myself what Mach 0.8 (or thereabouts) really felt like, plus the view from 47,000 ft. Or, to put it more graphically, the view of Earth some 8 miles below.

However, it was not all plain sailing for everyone. My good friend David Cobbold had a complete electrical failure as he turned into finals. He lost all his instruments and had to be talked down from the control tower. One of our Turkish colleagues had to make an emergency landing, wheels-up, somewhere in the far north, but the combination of wing tip-tanks (which usually carry fuel and can be ejected when empty) acting as skis and the frozen snow created a perfect artificial runway, together facilitating a textbook emergency landing. All these adventures gave everyone stories to tell, and we all learnt from the experiences. There were also the sadder stories, and much more mundane, like one poor colleague getting the chop because of repeated bouts of airsickness.

On 21 March 1957, I completed my last solo last flight. It was really just a spin, in total 1 hour 20 minutes, and not without a degree of sadness as I knew it marked the end of a phenomenal experience. However, I had been told that I was in the top quartile of pilots with particularly good solo navigation and instrument flying and I was cheered by the thought that I might become a

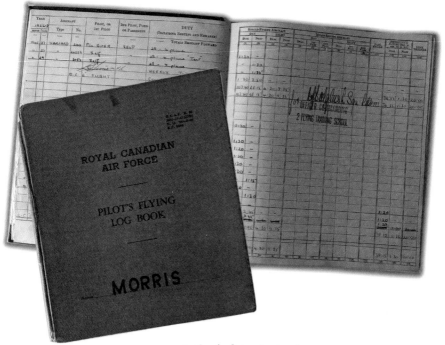

Author's flying logbook.

5517 course badge created by
David Cobbold and author.

Pathfinder! This was a role that applied to Bomber Command and usually involved Mosquitos flying at the front of a flying formation of bombers with the sole purpose of leading the way. The following day, I completed my final dual flight with my wonderful instructor Flying Officer Campbell which lasted 2 hours 30 minutes, carefully recorded in my logbook as, 'Mission #54 XCty OW'. Little did I know then that it would turn out to be my last ever flight in an RAF jet. My logbook records that I flew a total of 287 hours in the skies over RCAF MacDonald and snow-covered northern Canada, of which 120 hours were solo. What a thrill and privilege for any young man.

Whilst flying was our life, we four musketeers were still able to find time to relax. Having discovered the delights of the drive-in movies whilst at RCAF Moose Jaw, we continued with regular visits in MacDonald. One memorable evening, we were en route to the cinema with Ginger at the wheel, when the car somehow skidded off the road, down a snow-covered embankment, rolling ever so slowly and ending up upside down. Thankfully, no one was injured, so we all just got out to survey the scene. As jet-set pilots we were unfazed and so we gently rocked the car until it became upright, started the engine and managed to get back on the road. We even got to the movies as planned.

The Mess was also a popular hang-out where pilots could relax and share some quite outrageous stories. One sticks in my mind to this day. The story goes that one trainee pilot was out flying in the dark when he spied a train on the single-track heading west. He overtook the train and then turned the plane around, so it faced the oncoming train. He then dropped his undercarriage so that the landing lights came on and proceeded to fly straight at the train at full speed. The poor train driver had apoplexy at the sight of what he must have thought was another train coming directly at him on his single-track rail. Much screeching of brakes, then whoosh, the plane flew over him. I cannot mention the name as it may all have been made up, but I do wonder!

But enough of the frivolities; flying was completed and we had passed. We awaited our passing out parade, which was to take place on Saturday 24 March 1957, the highlight of which would be the presentation of our RAF Wings. Considering that our course included representatives from seven different nations, none of whom really liked drill work, the parade went well. Another bonus was that the ambient temperature was above freezing. But whatever technical skill we lacked on the parade ground we made up for in spirit in the Mess that evening as we celebrated in style. An evening never to be forgotten, and in a sense it was a double celebration as we had been told that, in a couple of weeks' time, we would be travelling home from Montreal on the SS *Empress of England*. I still have the photograph of the presentation of my Wings, which hangs proudly in my TV room. My RAF Wings badge is framed and sits alongside the 5517 course badge, together with my cut tie presented when I first 'went solo'. They are now over sixty-five years old, but the memories are as fresh as if it were yesterday.

Of the original four musketeers, we were now down to three, as John Robbins had signed on as a regular, which meant he had to go on a winter survival training course lasting two weeks. We remaining three travelled to Montreal to meet the SS *Empress of England* and were delighted to take possession of our cabins. As fully qualified pilot officers we were eligible to travel in First Class. How wonderful to be woken up with a tap on the door from the dedicated steward with morning tea.

However, none of the three of us, nor any of the rest of British pilots had any idea what would face us on reaching England. Rumours abounded that we might be sent to Cyprus as back-up for the Suez operation or we might go to a squadron, as our predecessors had done. Those were the exciting options. The more worrying rumours were that National Service Flying itself might be coming to end because of the Duncan Sandys Defence Review.

However, we revelled in the comforts of the SS *Empress of England*, one of the finest ocean liners of its day, noting the contrast to our outward voyage on the SS *Newfoundland*. Even the weather was different, and we travelled in calm seas. Little did we know just how fitting the expression 'the calm before the storm' would be for us, as what was in store would be anything but calm, and the subject of the next chapter.

Happy memories of comradeship.

CHAPTER TEN
GROUNDED – NATIONAL SERVICE ENDS

THE SS EMPRESS of England docked at Liverpool and we were met by an RAF Liaison Officer who issued us with First Class rail warrants to travel home. Mine was to my grandmother's house in Forest Hill, southeast London. He told us that we would receive our movement orders in two weeks' time but advised that we should expect some surprises as the whole of the RAF was under review by the government. This was chiefly due to the Defence White Paper of Duncan Sandys, which had recognised that the UK could no longer be a worldwide power, especially after Suez, and that there needed to be a change in defence strategy. As a result, the UK withdrew from positions east of Suez, and developed its nuclear-armed V bombers which would act as a major deterrent against Russia's nuclear weapons. Therefore, there would be a lesser need for the traditional fighter aircraft.

A week later the much-anticipated brown envelope dropped through the letterbox on to the doormat. I opened it as quickly and carefully as I could, hoping against hope that I was to join 601 Squadron at North Weald. I had had the foresight to contact them when I had finished at Kirton in Lindsey and had received an offer in principle from them. I had done my research and subsequently approached the Commanding Officer. For me, the squadron promised everything that I could wish for, and what a history it had. Stationed at North Weald, the base of 601 (County of London) Squadron, RAuxAF, was known as the 'Millionaires' Squadron' as it had been founded in White's Club in 1925 by Lord Edward Grosvenor. The squadron produced some of the greatest wartime heroes, including Roger Bushell, the leader of the famous 'Great Escape', cruelly murdered by the Nazis, as well as Billy Fiske, one of the first American pilots to die in the Second World.

But the envelope that arrived on my grandmother's doormat contained news which, for me, was quite devastating. It explained that there was to be no further aircrew selection for National Service. Those still in their training period, such as myself, would finish their course, but on getting their Wings they would be grounded to do general duties and there would be no more flying.

I immediately telephoned Brian and Tony to find out what was happening to them. Brian was posted on general duties at RAF Valley, which was a flying station at least, and he remembers enjoying some flying in a Vampire T11 as well as many rides in Ansons and air-sea rescue helicopters. Tony was posted to RAF Abingdon as Assistant Station Adjutant working in the Station Commander's outer office. He then went to Oxford to read Chemistry, where he was fortunate to be able to join the University Air Squadron and had a happy four years of flying Chipmunks. He then decided to re-join the RAF and had a long and distinguished career on Canberras and Vulcans. He reached the top with roles as Commanding Officer in the USA and Germany, and then a spell at the Ministry of Defence in London, before retiring in April 1990.

It is interesting to note the welcome Tony had from Oxford's University Air Service with the response that David Cobbold and I received at Cambridge, where the Commanding Officer was not at all interested in our offer of help and merely offered us social membership of the Mess. We declined.

As John Robbins had already made the switch and signed up as a regular, he was first posted to the 'Canadian Acclimatisation Course' and then to RAF Worksop to fly Vampires; hardly a challenge after the superior T33. However, he too went on to have a successful career in the RAF, mainly flying Hastings on long-range transport duties which took him around the world. He retired from the RAF in 1972, gained his civil flying licences, and flew Comets and Boeings for Dan-Air. For his final five years of service before retirement, he flew for British Aerospace as an instructor and test pilot.

My own specific instruction was to report to 54 MU (Maintenance Unit) at RAF Hucknall near Nottingham as General Duties Officer with specific responsibility for all housing accommodation for the many 'other ranks' personnel and their families. I was tasked to find accommodation, vet it, agree rentals and check our personnel in and out. It certainly did not present the same adrenaline-fuelled exhilaration of flying, but it did present its own challenges which, in turn, brought their own rewards. I did not know it at the time, but this was to be the start of a lifelong interest and commitment to the housing policy for our country, which has continued throughout my time in Parliament for nearly fifty years.

I arrived to be welcomed by the Flight Lieutenant Commanding Officer and the Flying Officer in charge of the recovery of crashed aircraft whose name was Steve; I was the third officer. RAF Hucknall, like all RAF bases, had had a colourful history and I took the time to find out a little about it in order to better understand my role and where I would fit in. This has become a central tenet to all my work ever since: it is always worthwhile to do a little research – on a place or a person or a company – so you can really make the best of any opportunity.

During the Second World War, RAF Hucknall had been the centre of Rolls-Royce's engine test flying. It also housed several RAF units. In September 1939, the airfield was listed as part of Fighter Command and the units were No. 98 (Battle) Squadron, a No. 2 Group Reserve Squadron and No. 1 (RAF) Ferry Pilots Pool in Maintenance Command. In March 1940 a Polish unit formed with thirty-one Battles, a two-seater plane which they used for training, and flying began on 14 April 1940. However, the unit was moved to Bramcote in June 1940. No. 1 Group HQ was evacuated from France in June 1940 and eventually came to stay at Hucknall until July 1941. One of the biggest challenges for the base during wartime was the arrival of more Polish units in January 1941, with lots of Tiger Moths, Battles and Oxfords, and then another arrived in July 1941, this time with Tiger Moths and Ansons, and they remained until the end of the war. After the war, the RAF continued to use part of the airfield for many years and among the units were No. 12 Group Communications Flight, No. 504 R Aux AF Squadron (Mosquito T3, NF 30, Spitfire F22) HQ No. 43 Group, Nottingham UAS, No.664 R Aux AF Squadron (Auster) and No. 54 MU.

When I arrived at RAF Hucknall in 1957, the airfield was still being leased to Rolls-Royce for its experimental test flying, particularly for its engine development. The RAF had sensibly given honorary membership of the Mess to all the pilots working at the test centre, so the Mess was never a dull place. Essentially, the maintenance units were handling a constant stream of broken or smashed aircraft which were either broken up for spares or just sold as metal. In RAF slang they were known as 'Crash & Smash Units'.

I soon settled in, with a nice bedroom in the Mess, delighted that I had a batman to look after all my domestic needs. I quickly decided I needed a small car, so with the help of Steve, I set about looking. We found a clean 1936 soft top Morris 8, the same age as myself, for £75. Thankfully, my dear girlfriend Ann, with whom I had been reunited, offered to make some new green seat covers which enhanced the vehicle enormously.

I became good friends with a Canadian test pilot who had a new 'souped up' MG Magnette; a beautiful, fast car. He went to London every weekend, offered me a lift which I enthusiastically accepted so that I could see Ann two out of three weekends as I had to do my share of work as Duty Officer. An amazing number of crashed aircraft would always arrive on Saturdays. The deal for the weekend London trips was to leave after work on Friday and be dropped off at Marble Arch, and then picked up again at 6.30pm on Sunday evening. I remember some lovely summer weekends when Ann and I would go to the Brevet Club for dinner and dancing on their postage stamp-sized dance floor.

Initially, the housing job was quite demanding and I enjoyed the challenges it presented. But then the news arrived that there were plans to close down the station, which would mean no new arrivals. In typical service fashion the authorities announced that there would still be an annual inspection. The Commanding Officer put me in charge and told me he wanted us to put on a really good show. He gave me the impossibly small budget of £25 and, I quote, 'to tart the place up'.

As luck would have it, Steve and I would sometimes drink at The White Post, outside Nottingham. One of the other regulars owned a plant nursery. On the spur of the moment, and I am not sure what gave me the idea, but perhaps it was the local brew, I asked him if it was possible to hire plants – I suggested geraniums. Much to my amazement, he agreed. He came down to the station, walked around and drew up a plan. He marked up a group of stones and ordered that they should all be painted white. He then said he would deliver and plant a whole load of geraniums the day before the inspection and would return the day after it to dig them up again. At first the Commanding Officer was incredulous, but then conceded and said, 'Michael, it's your show.' The day of the inspection arrived, the sun shone and what a sight to behold! The inspecting Wing Commander was impressed and said that it was the best station in his responsibility. He simply could not believe it had all been done for a mere £25. The Commanding Officer graciously said it was all down to yours truly, Pilot Officer Morris. The Wing Commander added that I should be flying and not landscaping, and as such he encouraged me to join the RAF on a PC (permanent commission) which he would support. I thanked him but said I had a place at St Catharine's College, Cambridge to read Economics. It reminded me that a Canadian Company had also offered me a post of aerial oil line inspecting, to which I had given the same answer.

With the inspection over, my final tasks were to organise the closing down dinner for Mess members and a special closing down ball. The dinner was a huge success with all the usual silly RAF games like getting round the edge of the room holding on to the picture rail without hitting the ground. All went well until my large Canadian friend pulled the picture rail down! But no matter, many more games followed, all accompanied by riotous singing which just proves that the best fun is self-made and does not have to cost anything. Just as well, as I was then summoned to a meeting with the Commanding Officer to plan the ball and was told there was no budget for it at all. However, he continued, he would be able to provide thirty-seven bottles of wine from the station cellar. They were not required to go back to the Air Ministry, as they were all corked. I was no expert in wine, but I knew enough to recognise that corked wine would be undrinkable. Before I could get a word of protest in, the Commanding Officer said, with a pronounced wink, that I must sign alongside his signature, confirming that all the bottles were corked, before adding, 'We shall drink the lot at our ball!' And we did. Ann and I have been to a number of Cambridge balls subsequently but the closing down ball at RAF Hucknall was truly special and Ann looked absolutely stunning in a green and white spotted ballgown that she had made herself. A poignant night, as it marked the end of a service career for many, myself included, and one which would never be forgotten.

A week later I drove out of RAF Hucknall for the last time to everyone's good wishes. Of course, there was a huge sadness that there had been no flying. Just think what a joy and privilege it would have been to be a part of 601 Squadron for six months. I can but envy my predecessor National Service Pilots who did join that squadron, even if they did only fly Vampires. Yet when I reflect on my time at Hucknall, I think of it fondly. Not only the friendships and camaraderie of station life, and the challenges of getting a job well done, but also the joy of going to my first ever Test Match at Trent Bridge when England played the West Indies. Those years in our late teens and early twenties are such formative ones and the experiences we have then really do shape our interests and skills for life. Watching cricket at Trent Bridge started a lifelong love of the game which would later see me become a member of the MCC, a captain of the Lords and Commons cricket team and, above all, President of Northamptonshire County Cricket Club.

Was this to be the end of my flying days? Certainly, for now as I was off to embark on the next adventure of my life at the University of Cambridge. Whether it was due to the wonderful flying I had enjoyed in Pakistan, in Canada and in the UK, or whether it was because I felt my flying experiences had been cut short due to no fault of my own, the deed was done and my love of flying had taken hold. My life would now take a very different route but flying would always remain a very special part of it.

CHAPTER ELEVEN
CHURCHILL'S MOST SECRET AIRFIELD

THIS CHAPTER IS not about National Service pilots but instead about a small airfield in the heart of Bedfordshire and its extraordinary wartime story. It warrants inclusion in this book as it played such a vital role in the fight against the Nazis by being the station from which Churchill's Special Operations Executive (SOE) agents left England to be dropped into occupied Europe, flown by brave airmen. As such, I believe their story deserves to be told. There are also several coincidences, or twists of fate, which clearly demonstrate just how closely linked we all our to our wartime ancestors and I do believe we should continue to salute their actions. The station was RAF Tempsford.

The catalyst to write this chapter was Remembrance Sunday, 8 November 2020, when Ann and I attended our local church, St Mary's, Everton. We do not actually live in the parish but when we moved to the outskirts of Sandy in 1973, we tried several local churches before settling on St Mary's where we both felt an inner harmony. We are on the electoral role, worship there reasonably regularly and all our family regard it as our parish church. Despite being the MP for Northampton South for just over twenty-three years, I have always visited St Mary's on Remembrance Sunday, as for me Sunday worship is a private and personal occasion and not one for politicking.

There we were, forced by Covid, to have the whole of the Remembrance Day service outside in the churchyard as the authorities had instructed that all churches were to be closed. Luckily it was a pleasant morning with no rain. As a former RAF pilot, albeit a National Service one, I was asked to lay a wreath, which I willingly accepted. The inscription on the card attached to the wreath read:

> In memory of all those brave men and women who gave their lives in the service of our country and particularly the aircrew and agents who flew from Tempsford airfield, never to return.
> The Rt Hon. the Lord Naseby PC – RAF National Service Pilot 1955–57

Gibraltar Barn,
RAF Tempsford.
(Richard Edwards)

Inside Gibraltar Barn,
RAF Tempsford.
(Richard Edwards)

One of many memorials inside Gibraltar Barn.
(Richard Edwards)

After the service, and in reflective mood, I took a walk around the churchyard. I looked again where I had looked so many times before but noted, with renewed interest, the graves of six aircrew who had died in the war years between 1942 and 1944. They had met their deaths on operations out of Tempsford in the valley just below the edge of the skyline as one faced north. I carefully read the inscriptions of all six but was moved when I noted that two of them were Canadians. Having got my Wings in Canada, I felt a particular affinity with them and wondered who they were and how they had come so far from their homeland to give their lives in service. I decided I would investigate further.

My knowledge of the airfield and its history had begun many years earlier when we first moved to Sandy, nearly four decades previously. Ann and I had decided to move our young family from Islington, north London where I had been Leader of the Council, as I had been chosen to fight for the Conservative Party for the seat of Northampton South. We wanted a larger house with grounds, but it needed to be convenient to get back to London as well as to the constituency. At that time, Ann worked as a GP in London and had half days on Wednesdays when she would often visit her mother in Bedford. We had found details of Caesar's Camp (an Iron Age hill fort) for sale in nearby Sandy and agreed she would have first look, on the next Wednesday, which she did. I followed on the Friday, en route for Northampton. We both liked the house and grounds and bought it in July 1973.

At that time, I knew little about RAF Tempsford, as I was busy with work and family, although I did notice that access to our house was via Sand Lane and I discovered it had been tarmacked during the war. I also noticed some old concrete huts at the end of the lane. Sometime later a conversation with a fellow local resident revealed that they had been used to house crew and ammunition for Tempsford. My curiosity was piqued, and I was keen to learn more, but it was not until a few years later, when I was chatting with Francis Pym who knew of my National Service record, that he suggested a visit to Gibraltar Barn. He explained that it was virtually all that remained of RAF Tempsford, except for parts of the concrete runways. Ann and I visited and were amazed at what we found: memorials to so many of the agents who flew out from Tempsford and their remarkable stories. It was a quiet place, one for reflection and we both felt moved by the accounts we read. They included a report on Odette Sansom (later Churchill), the famous SOE Agent who was dropped into enemy-occupied France to work with the Resistance. She was captured by the Nazis and taken to Ravensbrück concentration camp where she was tortured and only avoided death by using her quick wits to convince her captors she was related to Sir Winston Churchill.

But what of this little-known airfield that facilitated all these clandestine airdrops of agents and equipment? In truth, the history of RAF Tempsford, hidden away in the depth of east Bedfordshire was, for a long time, clouded in mystery. Undoubtedly, it was one of the key airfields of the Second World War, which began its official operations in October 1941 and continued until the disbandment of its last, and some would say core, squadron No. 161, on 2 June 1945. It even attracted the personal attention of Hitler himself, who ordered, 'find this viper's nest and obliterate it'. But the Germans were unsuccessful and never found it.

What did it do? It was brought into service to assist the Special Operations Executive, itself only created in 1940, tasked to organise clandestine flights into enemy territory in Europe and North Africa. The objective was to drop agents and supplies behind enemy lines, by parachute, before landing in the occupied territories to collect other agents and information and return them safely to England. All this under the cover of darkness. The missions were highly dangerous and often sabotaged. I recommend two fascinating books for those who want the detail of the story: Bernard O'Connor's *Churchill's Most Secret Airfield* and Hugh Verity's *We Landed by Moonlight*.

The Remembrance Day visit to the graves of the servicemen coincided with my initial research for this book, and I decided that I needed to visit Gibraltar Barn once again. I sought permission from my friend, the Earl Erroll, who owns the farm on which Gibraltar Barn lies. Today, the barn is still hidden away and has its roof but no doors. It is a strange and eerie place with just the sound of the wind interrupting the quietude and it is quite incredible to think the whole station was once home to 1,000 personnel and 200 buildings.

Back in the 1940s, there would have been another barn adjacent to the one still standing, where the agents would have been briefed on their mission and been issued with their kit. They would then have moved on to Gibraltar Barn for final checks to ensure that, in the event that they were caught or interrogated, they were not carrying anything that would give away their

British identity. The memorials and stories of these brave women and men recorded in pictures on the walls had me dumbfounded. Some were tortured, others abused and too often murdered. The majority of them very young girls: Violette Szabo, Denise Bloch and Joan Rolfe were all murdered at Ravensbrück Concentration camp in January 1945. There is a framed poem on the wall, written by Joan Munden née Rolfe:

> Don't leave a trace
> Don't trust anyone
> Remember each face
> Hide wireless and gun
>
> Code is your voice
> Silk is your tool
> Morse is your key
> A pianist, that's all
>
> Speak only French especially of love
> No English button or brand
> Your secret is mine, I'll still be here
> Though danger, torture, and ...
> We found your trace
> Your photo, your call
> We felt your courage transcend
> We came and stood where you died, not in vain
> We followed your trail to the end.

The agents were transported by aircraft housed at Tempsford, including Anson, Hudson, Whitley, Halifax, Sterling but possibly most especially by the Lysanders of 161 Squadron. Records show the squadron completed an impressive 266 sorties with 187 successes and only thirteen killed. The other aircraft were used for long range work. Overall, in the time it was operational, RAF Tempsford facilitated 1,643 sorties, 1,254 successes and fifty-two killed.

I am rather intrigued by the Lysander because it was a STOL (Short Take

Author's local church;
St Mary's, Everton
above RAF Tempsford.
(Richard Edwards)

The Lysander: the
workhorse used for
flying agents in and
out of France.
(Paul Ferguson, SVAS)

Aerial view of Churchill's most
secret airfield, RAF Tempsford.
(Richard Edwards)

Off and Landing) and was originally designed in 1936 – the year I was born. I recently visited the Shuttleworth Museum where they have just restored one and I was treated to a near hour-long briefing on its capabilities, many of which were included in its original design. What a cockpit! The pilot was able to see over the leading edge of the high lift wings, and its ability to land and take off in very short distances, in addition to its range of 1,100 nautical miles, made it perfect for trips to France and secret landings. Besides the pilot, there was space for two passengers in the fuselage and a modest amount of luggage, such as a radio kit. How I would love to be able to handle the controls. I won the 'landing on numbers' competition in Moose Jaw with the Harvard so I feel I was made for Lysander flying.

Inspired by my visits to Gibraltar Barn, I was determined to find out more about the two Canadian airmen buried in the graveyard at St Mary's. They were just two of a great number who came to Tempsford, from several allied countries, to join the fight again Hitler and his Nazis.

Pilot Officer Ian Wilson was twenty-five years old and single when he died. Before the war, he lived in Montreal and was an account executive for an advertising agency, the very same job I had when I was a similar age to him. He appears to have been on Squadron 138, flying Halifaxes. The second grave was for Leading Aircraftman Archibald Galbraith, from Toronto, who had volunteered in the first call as early as 1940. He had been a radio operator and must have served on both Whitleys and Halifaxes. I hope my few words here will help to keep their memory alive.

There is another memorial in Gibraltar Barn which reads:

This plaque commemorates the heroic deeds of the 157 men and 1 woman from the Polish Special Operations Executive
"Silent and Unseen"
CICHOCIEMNI
1942 – 1943
who flew from Tempsford in Halifax A/C to their top-secret missions. Dropped by parachute and resupplied by the brave British and Polish Airmen of No.138 (Special Duties) Squadron. They were key to Allied Operations.

The Poles' incredible service record has been well documented, and I now have a Polish daughter-in-law, Ola, whom I greatly admire. We are all indebted to the bravery and sacrifices made by so many during that global conflict and a visit to Gibraltar Barn always reminds me just how much my own life story is linked to those who gave their lives. Perhaps one final story here will serve to illustrate this most clearly.

When I worked as Marketing Manager for Reckitt & Colman Ceylon, I soon discovered that my boss in Colombo had been in the RAF during the Second World War. We had that shared bond, but he always refused to divulge where or what he had flown: 'Sorry Michael, Official Secrets Act.' I left Ceylon in 1963. In 1973 the family moved out of London to Sandy and the following Christmas I sent Alex a card with my new address. Back came his card with the following: 'Know the area well, particularly Tempsford – enough said! Alex.'

When I visited the Shuttleworth Museum to see the Lysander, I was given a talk by a former pilot, Jim Box, and I mentioned my old boss, Alexander. 'Yes,' said Jim, 'he flew several times and we have records of some of his missions':

> Flg Off G.J.F. Alexander. 6/7 May 44 Operation SILENE Pierrot, Location Outarville; Out 'equipment only' Home (3) XP12 Fanfouet, Mahurin (USAAF Major):
> source p.222, *We Landed by Moonlight*, Hugh Verity.
> Flg Off Alexander 4/5 Aug 44, Double Lysander, Operation Scimitar, Location of field La Chartre sur Loire Field 'L22', Out passengers 3: Paule – Denise, Corre and a British Pilot. Return Man and Woman Remarks Alexander's Lysander damaged in landing. Returned in fog to St Eval.

Thinking of the colleague and friend I once knew, I dug a little deeper to find out more. I wonder what it must have been like on that clear moonlit night for a pilot armed with just a map trying to find a particular field somewhere along the Loire in southwest France. I discover that this was to be no normal SOE operation: Alex was shot at by light flak and forced to land. I found his Commander's Report and quote from it:

At approximately 0200 on 6 Aug I landed on ground L22. From the air the ground seemed excellent. I touched down on stubble but on coming up level with lamps 'b' and 'c' ran into a narrow belt of standing crop.

I read on, fascinated, as the saga continued: he hit more stubble, uncut cereals and bundles of hay, resulting in the tail wheel being badly damaged. At normal taxing power the damaged tail wheel made the Lysander go round in a small circle, so he had use full throttle to manoeuvre; additionally, his elevator was damaged, so he had to fly home on his trimmer. His stick only controlled the ailerons – it could only move fore and aft. Finally, to cap it all, his aerials were damaged, so he had to fly home with no radio to somewhere in southwest England covered in morning fog. By sheer chance he found RAF St Merryn. He landed just as the local Liberators had taken to the sky.

He had collected two agents: a man and a girl with a broken hip. He left them in the plane to go and find help. He walked in plain clothes for nearly two hours before finding the control tower of the station and was taken to the station's Commanding Officer. Alex went back to the Lysander in the Commanding Officer's car and found his two passengers deeply entwined on the floor of their section! Such is the versatility of the Lysander.

Well, to say I was flabbergasted by the whole story is a total understatement. It just goes to show never be afraid to ask, to dig and keep digging if the cause warrants.

As one walks out of Gibraltar Barn, one notices six trees planted nearby in front of the barn. On closer inspection, one notes that the trees come from six different countries, each country having provided service crew for operations from Tempsford. Planted as saplings to remember the fallen, today they are each a tall tree, reaching for the sky, as those who they represent did, night after night. A truly majestic memorial to those who gave their lives in service and a beautiful one to be appreciated by those who visit.

I do believe that Gibraltar Barn and the two surviving sheds which are home to so much important memorabilia are too precious to be kept virtually out of sight. I very much hope that the RAF Association, together with the co-operation of the Erroll family and possibly a grant from the National Lottery, will one day create a proper museum on the site. This will require sensitivity and understanding from all involved, but I earnestly believe it can and should be done in order that we never forget the sacrifices that were made. I am sure that such a plan would have support from government, as there is continuing interest in flying in Parliament, not least from those who have licences to fly. I am not the only one who did National Service in the RAF. My research shows there are four others listed: Lord Pendry, Lord Renfew, Lord Soley and Lord Sterling.

There is also an active All-Party Parliamentary Group on General Aviation chaired by Lord Davies of Gower, of which I am a member. At present we are focusing on how we can ensure that our heritage aircraft are looked after. We propose that the government should do more to safeguard the important remaining examples of historic aircraft nationwide through the creation of a national collection like the scheme already in place for naval vessels. It seems a natural continuation of this conversation to discuss the preservation of the stations that housed these aircraft and the memory of those who worked at them. As such, my final tribute is to Alex, the two Canadian serviceman, the 158 Poles and every other pilot who flew out of Tempsford, and the words that are written, without a source, on the walls of Gibraltar Barn: 'The brave never die; they live on in history forever.'

CHAPTER TWELVE
FLYING IN THE BLOOD

Here am I, at the time of writing eighty-five years of age, still enthralled with flying and by all those who have flown and continue to fly. There is no doubt that the desire to master the skies has led to one of mankind's greatest achievements and so it was ever thus from the first flight in a balloon in 1780. It took more than another one hundred years before we saw the first powered flight, that of the Wright Brothers, but then the pace of progress quickened enormously. Over the following one hundred years we saw the development of powered flight, beginning with journeys across the English Channel, then across the Atlantic Ocean and on to flights around the entire globe. The flying machines which facilitated these flights developed from balloons to zeppelins, then powered aircraft to jet propulsion. Today, with the globe conquered, we are reaching for the stars with the development of rocket propulsion and space tourism, and just round the corner is the brave new world of hydrogen power.

For me, the personal catalyst for this lifelong fascination was the bombing of Dolphin Square by German Bombers in 1940, which forced my evacuation to Bromyard in Herefordshire. This was followed by a move in 1943 to Pinner, Middlesex and prep school at St John's School, Pinner where we schoolboys played around with paper darts and experienced the V1 rockets which I remember seeing from my garden in about 1944.

My interest was further heightened when I joined Bedford School in January 1950 and heard about nearby RAF Cardington. We didn't know much about it, but schoolboy gossip informed me that it was home to 'balloons'. Nobody really knew what went on there, which only served to arouse my teenage curiosity even more. It seems strange to think that I spent a week there, in an official capacity, on my way to Kirton in Lindsey at the beginning of my National Service and it feels appropriate to now share a little of what has gone on and continues to go on there.

Cardington started out as an airship station run by the Short Brothers who had an office in Bedford in the early part of the twentieth century. Construction started on the first shed at the station in 1916 and its first airship, R31, was built by 1918. The last rigid airship was the fated R101 which crashed on 5 October 1930 near Beauvais, France killing all the passengers during its maiden voyage to India. Such was the importance of this voyage that on board were Lord Thomson, the Air Minister and Sir William Sefton Brancker KCB, AFC, an Old Boy of Bedford School. He himself was a noted pioneer of civil and military aviation; he had flown in the First World War and worked his way through a myriad of promotions up through the ranks of both the RAF, and the civil service. In 1924, on his retirement from the RAF he was granted the rank of Air Vice Marshal. I find it both strange and sad that such a tragedy is so little known today. Compared to that other famous maiden voyage, that of the *Titanic*, it is even stranger that this pioneering development in the air industry has been so overlooked and forgotten. It may seem like a quaint and tame mode of transport today, but this tragic accident shows just how dangerous these early aircraft were and how brave were those who chose to travel in them.

The other key role of Cardington was as the headquarters for Government Balloon Operations and which from 1938 until 1984 were primarily used for metrological research, although not exclusively as interest in airships continued. The 1970s brought Mr Smith's airship 'Santos Dumont' G-BAWL (1974), which had a chequered life but no doubt paved the way for the first truly modern airship, the Skyship 500 G – BECE, built in 1979 by Airship Developments. There followed another fifteen ships, of both 500 and 600 models, and these flew successfully all over the world and carried passengers too. The last airship flight from Cardington was the Airlander prototype which took place on 17 November 2017, and which is discussed in more detail in the penultimate chapter.

It seems only right that RAF Cardington and the amazing work that has happened there has a place in this book, as it has no doubt played an important part in my lifelong love of flying and fascination with aviation. A few other memorable experiences of flying and aviation in my life after National Service spring to mind.

In the late 1960s, when I worked in advertising, I had to travel a few times to Paris. On one flight with BEA, approaching Paris Orly airport, the front nose wheel would not lock. An aircraft came up and tried to nudge the wheel with its wing tip but to no avail. This was a dangerous operation but certainly the lesser of the evils, and eventually, we, the passengers were told by the captain in a calm voice to prepare for a crash landing. I was selected to hold one side of the escape shoot rope as we landed on a foam-covered runway. The minute the plane came to a halt the door was opened and I jumped down and pulled on the rope to inflate a slide for the passengers to slide down. All went well until two Japanese passengers leapt into the shoot still carrying their duty free (they had been told to leave behind)! Result: total chaos and a sea of vodka!

On a parliamentary visit to Namibia, four of us, including the pilot, took off from Windhoek in a light plane. As the only former pilot I sat in the front with the pilot, relishing the opportunity to be up close and personal with the instruments in the cockpit. After we had levelled off, I suggested we might go a little lower to see the wonderful safari animals below. At the time, there were anti-South African government terrorists in Angola, who were being funded by the Russians, but this felt a long way away from politics as we admired the beautiful countryside below. However, the pilot's answer came back loud and clear: 'No sir, at this level we are above small arms fire but below the level of the SAM-7 missiles!'

A few years later, I flew on a Garuda airliner en route to Indonesia over Kuwait. I asked to go to the cockpit to have a clearer look at the ground, as my eldest son Julian was a major in the RAMC in the frontline in the First Gulf War. From the cockpit, I could see so clearly the deployment of the NATO forces down below. Obviously, my son was not visible to me, or me to him, but it felt good to see where he was. It also reminded me just what a complete game-changer aircraft are in warfare because of the panoramic view they afford.

In August 1992, I was asked by the then Speaker of the Commons, the Rt Hon. Betty Boothroyd MP in my role as her senior deputy to represent Parliament at the tenth anniversary celebrations of the recapture of the Falkland Islands from Argentina, which saw them returned to British sovereignty. I flew out of Brize Norton with a few other dignitaries. We refuelled at Ascension Island, where I was immediately approached by the Chairman of the Ascension Island Golf Club. Would I as President of the Lords and Commons Parliamentary Golf Society please come and re-open their restored club by driving a ball off the first tee? I hate the first drive but all went well and we continued with our journey. On the plane, I had the very great pleasure of sitting next to Terry Waite who was representing the Archbishop of Canterbury. He really is a truly remarkable man and I was grateful for the long flight so that I could speak to him at length.

Following the devastating tsunami of Boxing Day 2004, my wife Ann and I flew out to the Maldives and Sri Lanka to see how we could help. I was Chairman of both All-Party Parliamentary Groups and Ann a doctor, so we felt sure there was much that we could do. We arrived in Malé and were briefed on the biggest problem facing the majority of the islands, which was that the power generators had been knocked out by sea water. There were hardly any local engineers available and so I telephoned our High Commissioner in Colombo and asked him to request assistance from our Royal Navy ships that were positioned off Trincomalee. More specifically, I asked how many electrical engineers they could spare from the ships who could be deployed to get the generators up and running. From memory it was eight but the High Commissioner reminded me that many of the islands were deemed 'dry countries' where alcohol was not available and British engineers would need alcohol to keep them going. My next challenge was to persuade the President. We had a meeting and I asked him directly: 'Is it a deal that the Royal Navy men can have alcohol?' The answer was emphatic: 'This is a national emergency and so, yes!'

I did some further work travelling by an Otter seaplane, which afforded us some striking views of the devastation below. I was particularly struck by the sight of fish swimming in a pond right in the middle of an island. So great had been the force of the tsunami that they had been carried from the seashore all the way inland.

On another occasion in Sri Lanka, I was accompanying the President on a helicopter flight to Anuradhapura. We were flying just above the cloud base when the pilot announced in an agitated voice that he could not see the ground and had lost radio contact. I was seated on the port side and looked out of the window. Years of flying had taught me to look for landmarks by which to navigate. I noticed the pinnacle of a *stopa* (rather like a cathedral's spire but belonging to an Islamic building), which I pointed out to the President. He recognised it immediately and advised the pilot that there were grass fields to the north of the temple. The pilot descended through the cloud and thankfully the President had been right: we came into a smooth landing on grass, much relieved that our combined knowledge of the country below had helped us through a potentially difficult situation.

I will also never forget being lucky enough to witness, from the ground, one of Concorde's last flights. It happened to coincide with the Wimbledon Tennis Championships, which as a member I always attend, and as she roared over us, she was met with a similar roar of appreciation from the crowds below. It was a truly magical moment so perfectly captured in photographs which continue to remind us what a truly great aircraft she was and allow us time to reflect on the part Concorde has played in the story of aviation.

Concorde flying over Wimbledon on one of her last flights,
Sunday 6 July 2003. (AELTC/James Lipman)

However, for me the occasion which affords the best opportunity to reflect on bigger history of aviation and more specifically about the history of the RAF and its wartime record, is the annual Battle of Britain Memorial service, usually held at Westminster Abbey. This is a specific, dedicated day to reflect on the RAF and the sacrifice of those young pilots who saved our country in our hour of need. The 2020 event, held in the middle of the Covid-19 crisis had particular poignancy, as fewer than one hundred people were allowed to attend. The usual attendance is around 2,000. Fittingly, the Prime Minister read the lesson as three Spitfires and a Hurricane flew over. On 15 September, a larger crowd assembled to visit the Battle of Britain Memorial on the Embankment in London, not far downstream from the Houses of Parliament. Which just goes to show the high regard our nation has for its fallen heroes and particularly those who served in the skies.

Today, I am fortunate that I do not really have to go anywhere to be reminded of my time as a pilot. My home in Sandy, Bedfordshire is at the end of the 'green sand ridge' on the site of an ancient fort, dating back to before the Romans, overlooking the River Ivel. As such, it is a key landmark for aircraft. I can sit on our terrace and hear the roar of the Red Arrows or a fly-past to commemorate the Battle of Britain with the distinctive engine beat of the Lancaster Bomber. I can also recognise the interwar aircraft from nearby RAF Shuttleworth. I even find it uplifting to be working in the large kitchen garden and to suddenly hear the engine noise of some aircraft. Quite often my dog Biggles and I will take a short rest on my MCC bench just to look up to see what is going on and to reflect on my own experiences up there in the skies.

CHAPTER THIRTEEN
FIFTY-YEAR REUNION

PEOPLE REALLY LOOK forward to any reunion, although the majority of them are regular events, held annually or to mark a specific anniversary: five years, ten years, twenty years, etc. It is rare to have any to do with National Service and I can only think this is because so much time has now passed since we were active recruits. However, I was delighted when I got news of a possible reunion for RAF course 5517. It was all the brainchild of my friend David Cobbold who was also on course 5517 and a friend of his, Graham Jenkins, from a later course, 5606. It was to celebrate the fiftieth anniversary of our flying training in Canada at Moose Jaw and Macdonald.

So it was on 30 December 2005 that, together with another seven former National Service pilots who had trained in Canada, I received a very special email. I already knew it was coming, as David and I had discussed its contents in the House of Lords where we both found ourselves, he as a Hereditary Peer and I appointed by Prime Minister Tony Blair after my twenty-three years in the House of Commons: my final five years as Deputy Speaker and Chairman of Ways and Means responsible for the Maastricht Bill's stormy passage through the House of Commons. I told David it was a wonderful idea which I would fully support. Like all good events, this would require some careful planning, but David had already made a start, as he explained in his email:

> The Plan is to earmark the weekend of 1st/2nd July 2006 and to focus on a gathering at Shuttleworth Collection at Old Warden Airfield, Bedfordshire. They have their summer flying display on Sunday 2nd. Tony Haigh Thomas who runs the collection is a personal friend and still flies jets although he did not train in Canada. He is enthusiastic and believes he can organise a Harvard and maybe a T33. We can use their catering facilities and take a picnic – at least to watch a fly-by!

He added that he had put an advertisement in the January–March edition of

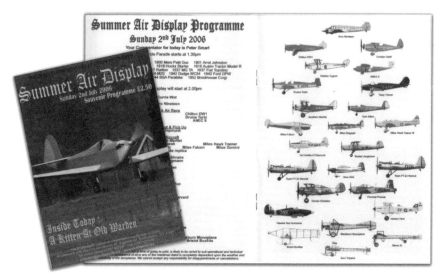

Programme from the fiftieth anniversary reunion.

The Harvard – a
wonderful memory.
(Paul Ferguson, SVAS)

The T33 in a
wonderful display.
(Darren Harbar)

the RAF Association's *Airmail* magazine in the reunions section.

I was thrilled to see that the email had also been sent to my former roommates Tony Collins and John Robbins. I quickly sent my own email with the plans to Brian Stevens – the fourth musketeer – with whom I had re-made contact. He was now living in Brazil and busy building fibreglass boats. The wonders of modern communication; email and the internet has allowed us to reconnect with so many people, it is a truly remarkable thing.

In January, David was in touch again and this time he proposed that the invitation should be extended to families and that wives, children and of course grandchildren should also attend. We discussed whether we should include other courses and decided that we should. Fifty years was a very special number and we wanted this to be a real celebration. There was also discussion about whether the venue should be North Weald (where I was originally scheduled to go) as they had a Harvard and a grounded T33 but it was dismissed as we were really keen to get a flying T33 if at all possible.

Over the following weeks, we continued to liaise but essentially David was organising the show and by mid-March the numbers had begun to swell. The notice in *Airmail* had yielded a good response and we even had replies from some former colleagues who now lived overseas. The idea had been met with unanimous favour and everyone was enthusiastic.

The plan took shape and, thankfully, the man in charge of the Shuttleworth Collection, Tony Haigh Thomas, who was a friend of David's, really did come up trumps. He said there was both a Harvard and a T33 at Duxford, Cambridge which was just ten minutes' flying time from Shuttleworth and therefore he thought it ought to be possible to include both aircraft in the summer show on 2 July. David then wrote to John Romain of the Aircraft Restoration Company at the Imperial War Museum, Duxford asking if they would allow the Harvard and T33 to take part in the Old Warden summer display. There followed a bit of a wobble as people began to wonder if we should move the whole show to Duxford, but I was not at all keen. David pressed on with his enquiries and got in touch with Anna MacDowell at Duxford. She confirmed all would be well, as the T33 was booked to attend an air show in Belgium on 2 July and so it could still do a fly-past with some aerobatics on its return journey. Perfect! And so a few days later it was confirmed that both aircraft, the Harvard and the T33, would take part, although only the Harvard would land at our celebratory show. The acceptance emails kept coming in: John J. Noble, course 5303, from Switzerland and President of the Geneva Flying Club accepted and also provided yet more names. Graham Jenkins emailed from Cyprus to say that six of his course were hoping to attend and with their families too. I had been trying to contact Rene Rouby in France and Barry Mawson in Canada but so far had had no response. It is quite remarkable how the bond of friendship between flyers from eight different NATO countries has lasted for fifty years. Of the four musketeers, there would be three of us attending, with our wives: Tony Collins, John Robbins and I. Sadly Brian Stevens, living in Brazil, could not make it, but sent word that he would be thinking of us all. David and his wife Chryssie kindly invited everyone signed up for the Sunday to also attend a garden party at their home on the Saturday evening. The party was to take place in the garden terrace room next to the entrance to Knebworth House. As there was also a wedding taking place there that day, we were assured a jolly atmosphere, as the wedding party had also booked a band.

At last the great day arrived – Sunday 2 July 2006 – which coincided with the celebration for the 66th Anniversary of the Battle of Britain. The sun was shining and there was no cloud; ideal conditions for watching aircraft going through their paces in the sky above. Our party had a marquee perfectly positioned so we could have an uninterrupted view, and consisted of thirty-nine former pilots from ten different courses with no less than six from overseas – namely Canada, New Zealand, Switzerland, Cyprus and Australia. Truly remarkable. We were all wonderfully supported by twenty-nine wives and partners, plus David had somehow managed to acquire a mannequin fitted out in an old flying officer's uniform. It was a great gathering.

The flying was not scheduled to start before 13:30 hrs, which allowed us plenty of time to catch up on old friendships, savour the atmosphere and lubricate ourselves for the show. We were briefed by the organiser that the Air Traffic Zone around Old Warden was 2 nautical miles radius and 2,000 ft vertically. The Old Warden control tower was fully manned to ensure proper air traffic control and additionally to communicate with spectators, like us, on 130Mhz. These were the frequencies used by pilots to communicate with each other in the air, but it was wonderful for us veterans to be able to tune in and listen too.

David Cobbold, chief organiser with a mannequin.

All the former pilots (author in red trousers).

We four: Brian (Ginger), author, John and Tony, reunited a few years after the fifty-year reunion.

Since it was a summer show there were several gimmicks for the assembled crowds, including a mock air race and a Chipmunk doing ribbon-cutting and pick-ups. This is always fun to watch: two poles are placed in the ground with a ribbon tied across between them. The Chipmunk swoops down with its wheels down and flies between the two poles and cuts the ribbon with its wheels as it passes. The serious flying started at 14:07 hrs with an Avro 19. There followed about half a dozen other classic aircraft before the Miles Hawk and then the gallant Gloucester Gladiator took their turn. At around 15:50 hrs we could hear a Spitfire Mk26 revving its engine, ready for take-off at 15:56 hrs for a flight lasting just six minutes. However, it was time enough for it to complete several low passes as well as a steep climb with a stall turn at the apex. I cannot imagine there was anyone present there, hearing its imitable sound and seeing it fly past, who did not immediately think of the Battle of Britain. The very name of the Spitfire is synonymous with it.

By this time our group was all on high alert and on tenterhooks. The noise of the Spitfire had stirred up our emotions and we knew that the time allocated to our beloved Harvard and T33 was fast approaching. The Harvard had been billed as a '1940s trainer' which seemed pretty hard on all of us who flew it in the late 1950s! And then, from the southern end of the runway, we heard the growl of the brutish radial engine and suddenly to our right it appeared: 'the yellow peril' (the colour of all primary trainers), in all its rugged form. It did a good display of aerobatics and I reflected it must have had all the characteristics of a plane capable of almost anything. It had been a Harvard that Neil Williams trained on in our course 5517 and he had gone on to become World Aerobatic Champion. Then over the intercom we were asked to look to our right again as, dead on time at 16:28 hrs and all the way from Belgium, the beautifully sleek T33 appeared. It was powered by its Rolls-Royce Nene engine and its red wing tip tanks glistened in the sunshine. There was total silence from the crowd of several thousand people, no doubt awestruck as the pilot took the aircraft through its paces in the sky above. There was nostalgia allied to fixation from all thirty-nine former pilots, each of us with our own, special memories of handling this beautiful piece of machinery, with no vices, fifty years previously. The scheduled seven minutes took ten – the pilot indulged us – and on the final run low over the runway, the wings were tipped in salute to all of us pilots who had flown in this beautiful, potentially devastating, aircraft. In the air show programme, the public was informed that this was 'a classic 1950s jet', but to we thirty-nine, she was our beloved T-bird.

She flew off to the east on her return to Duxford and, by a cruel twist of fate, she would never again be flown in front of such a large audience. Sadly, the T33 crashed at Duxford on 6 September 2006 and was totally destroyed. It was a Canadair made T33, ex-RCAF 21261 but then registered as G-TBRD and owned by Golden Apple Operations. It is so easy to feel invincible up in the skies, but this crash reminds us all that it really is a miracle that man has conquered the skies and these ageing aircraft still deserve and demand the utmost respect. Thankfully, as we packed up none of us knew of this impending disaster.

What a day to remember; indeed, what a weekend. I was delighted that course 5517 had the largest numbers of attendees but there were also former pilots from 5301, 5303, 5316, 5515, 5516, 5606, 5616 and 5705: an amazing number really. Not long after the thank you letters came flooding in, including one from the Shuttleworth Trust thanking us all for the donation of £500. David sent several emails and his words, I am sure, echoed the feelings of us all:

> ... very much enjoyed the weekend and meeting old friends and new. Luckily we were blessed with perfect weather. The climax of the Harvard and T33 really did bring tears to the eyes.

David wrote to us all again that Christmas, reminding those of us on course 5517 that it had been fifty years previously that we had been at RCAF MacDonald 'making friends with the T- Birds. What an experience to treasure.' I could not have agreed more and did wonder if I would ever get to experience anything remotely similar again. Thankfully, I did, although I had to wait another decade before the opportunity arrived.

In 2017, on the occasion of my eightieth birthday, my family and I went to Duxford Airfield and Museum where they had booked an hour-long flight in a Tiger Moth DH82A. It is a flight I shall never forget. Because of insurance rules I was not allowed to do the take-off or landing, but I nevertheless enjoyed over thirty minutes in control with just the one comment from my instructor, 'nose up a notch'. My logbook records '40 minute trial flight dual with P. Hughes' and the comment, 'Superb'. We managed to get permission to fly down the runway at Shuttleworth where I am a life member and then fly over to my home, Caesar's Camp, circling it several times, and all recorded on a video camera for posterity! I found it remarkable that after sixty years I could take the controls and my fingers had lost none of their light touch.

Is this to be the last time? It all depends on how the body bears up, but my ninetieth birthday is only five years away, at the time of writing, and, as this chapter has shown, everyone loves a reunion. Just as a reminder to my fellow National Service pilots, I give you the second verse of RCAF Pilot Officer Magee's poem and emphasise the last line.

> Up, up the long, delirious, burning blue
> I've topped the wind-swept heights with easy grace
> Where never lark nor ever eagle flew
> And, while with silent lifting mind I've trod
> The high untrespassed sanctity of space,
> Put out my hand, touched the face of God.

CHAPTER FOURTEEN
THE FUTURE OF AVIATION

IN MANY WAYS this is the most difficult chapter to write, due to the importance of the aviation industry to the world economy set against the impact of carbon emissions on climate change and the UK's target to reach net zero emissions by 2050.

I am a marketing man by profession. I studied Economics at St Catharine's College, Cambridge, obtaining an upper second in the Tripos of 1960. I joined the Reckitt & Colman Group (now Reckitt Benckiser) as a trainee, was posted to India and then to Ceylon (as it was called before it became Sri Lanka in 1972), by which time I was the Marketing Manager for the company. After nearly five years, I changed horses by joining an advertising agency, ending up as Senior Director of Benton & Bowles, which at the time was the fifth largest advertising agency in the world. This was in the 1960s and 1970s, and even then international travel was very much part of the job and I would have been one of many who would travel around the globe for work. This trend has only continued as time has passed and I am in no doubt that the demand to fly will increase again once the Covid-19 crisis is brought under control. The use of Zoom and Teams and other methods of communication has had a dramatic impact, but each of them has downsides. Once people are free to fly again, I believe demand will return to its upward curve, because although Zoom in particular is a good vehicle for some international discussions, it cannot provide the chemistry that comes from the personal interaction of face-to-face meetings. Just as an aside, I well remember one summer my wife, a GP, the children and I spent our two weeks' hard-earned holiday in our cottage in Suffolk. It rained almost every day. Afterwards Ann said to me, 'Your job for next year is to find the sun!' Every man knows his wife is to be obeyed and I set to work: the following year we did find the sun, in the south of France. My conclusion is that while the concept of 'staycation' has been reasonably successful, given half a chance many people will want to fly to find the sun for their summer holidays.

In recent years, I have been to a number of briefings about achieving net

The Airlander: the modern queen of airships. (Hybrid Air Vehicles)

zero emissions in the aviation sector. I was impressed by the briefing from Rolls-Royce, held in the summer of 2021, and quote from their background briefing document received after the outline welcoming speech, as it puts matters into context.

Aviation is a force for good in modern society, underpinning trade, commerce, connectivity and intercultural understanding. Aviation and aerospace are complex, interconnected global industries and ultimately operate at a systems level. Carbon emissions (CO_2) from aviation represented 2.6 per cent of total global emissions prior to Covid-19, although this proportion is expected to rise, as other sectors where solutions are more easily scalable decarbonise more rapidly; a challenge which the industry is strongly committed to addressing. The UK has significant competitive advantage through established R&T [research and technology] and innovation ecosystem in aerospace which it can use to develop the jet zero technologies of the future based on the transformative capacity of science and technology. Additionally, this represents a significant export opportunity for the UK.

The question is, what is 'jet zero' and 'innovation ecosystem'? And are they realistically achievable, and if so, in what timescale? There are several important contributing factors to consider.

Domestic aviation

This is an area that is readily developable because net zero technologies can be deployed without requiring major infrastructure. This is because UK airports can already accommodate both big and small passenger aircraft: small, domestic aircraft have smaller engines, which can be adapted more easily than larger ones. Countries in the developing world may not have the same resources and budgets available. There are partners already working on the short-haul market, such as Vertical Aerospace of Bristol, as well as Rolls-Royce with funding from the British Government via the Aerospace Technology Institute (ATI). The British Government has set an objective to achieve this by 2040 but it will need to be careful that, should domestic flights be curtailed, it is not undermined by non-UK routes taking a market share into UK inbound destinations. This sub-sector of the aviation industry is an ideal test market for new investment for research and development, but there must be a clear roadmap which outlines its objectives.

Sustainable Aviation Fuels (SAF)

There is a huge amount of work going on to replace fossil-based fuels that would require no significant changes to aircraft or to airports, which would be amazing. Coupled with this is the work by Rolls-Royce to produce an aero-engine called the Ultra Fan, as well as their new, experimental, electrically powered aircraft, the 'Spirit of Innovation'. It is powered by a 400 KW (500hp) motor with a battery pack that Rolls-Royce says has the best power density of any used in aviation. There must have been cheers at Rolls-Royce's headquarters when they tested this new machine which averaged 345 mph over 3 km, beating the existing record set by a Siemens aircraft by an incredible 132 mph. This took place on 20 November 2021 and the results were ratified in January 2022 by the Fédération Aéronautique Internationale. Of course, the age-old problem of bridging the gap between ambition and affordability continues to plague these pioneering efforts. One known bottleneck is the need for a constant supply of reliable, highly

Rolls-Royce Spirit of Innovation – another first for Britain. (John M. Dibbs)

secure, low carbon such as could come from small modular reactors. Maybe after the fuel price scares and shortages of September/October 2021, the British Government will be forced to sit up and listen. Having worked in the marketing world I do believe that test markets are absolutely vital in developing any new product, regardless of whether it is a consumer product or, in this case, specialist processes in the STEM industries. I also believe that the MOD and the RAF have a crucial role to play in testing and evaluating these processes and products in real life scenarios.

Development of zero-emissions flight in the UK

There clearly is no single bullet to the decarbonisation of aviation. There needs to be a continual and sustained investment in aerospace technologies through the ATI. The ATI's support is possibly the single most important means of meeting the ambitions needed and I am sure Rolls-Royce would probably agree. I have mentioned and sourced a good deal of my material from Rolls-Royce, not just out of loyalty to my first jet, the T33 Silver Star Trainer with its Rolls-Royce Nene engine rather than its original US Allison thereby increasing its performance all round. But primarily because wisely the UK Government holds a golden share. When one considers all the different areas that Rolls-Royce is working in, including fuel cells, hybrid and micro-electric grids and the small modular reactor to mention a few, it gives me great hope that we will achieve our objectives. It is also wonderful to see this company is now motoring again and how good to read that it has been awarded the engine contract for the US Air Forces B-52 Bombers worth up to $2.6 bn (£1.9bn).

Greenhouse gas removal

It is important that the government keeps abreast of developments in all sectors to ensure there is benefit and possible application in other industries too. Direct Air Capture is a good example which appears to offer a medium- to long-term route to de-coupling economic growth from increasing emissions. It is also important that the green taxonomy, deployed by the government to assist companies working to find solutions to the emissions question, applies to any and all companies doing pioneering or development work, not just those working in the aviation sector. This requires a joined-up approach across different industries to ensure maximum opportunity for investment and support from both the public and private sectors.

Non-CO$_2$ impacts on aviation

This is a challenging subject, as the overall footprint of aviation is not fully understood; indeed, climate scientists are still grappling with it. The really important point is that where the international community reaches agreements on mechanisms to address non-CO$_2$ impacts, the UK must stay involved and support further ongoing work. This particularly applies to the Advanced Contact Intelligence Organisation at international level. There are bound to be novel propulsion and fuel technologies that could have an impact on non-CO$_2$ impacts which will have to be understood and quantified before being adopted.

So, who is actually doing this valuable and important investigative work? The simple answer is, quite a large number of people, which augurs well. I have already mentioned the work of Rolls-Royce, which is at the forefront of many of the relevant conversations. Airbus is testing an aircraft that burns liquid hydrogen in modified gas turbine engines. Boeing is keeping pretty quiet, but one suspects it must be searching. Nearer to home, BAE Systems is known to be working quietly on something thought to be highly relevant.

There are also smaller companies, like the Canadian firm Carbon Engineering, conducting useful research, as well as Lanza Tech UK, backed by British Airways and Virgin Atlantic. It is great to hear that our commercial aviation giants are investing in research to find solutions. There is a US company, Ampaire, which has designed a battery-driven propeller and fitted it to a Cessna Skymaster that is actually flying in the UK. Extensive work is going on at Cranfield University where Zero Avia has already raised money to fund another useful project: the design and build of a small commercial aircraft powered by a hydrogen fuel cell. It had its first flight in September 2021. Now it is also working on a Dornier 228. Zero Avia is to be taken seriously because it is going straight for fuel cells. In this case its objective is to retrofit existing aircraft with new hydrogen engines. These units turn hydrogen into electricity which turns a propeller. One might ask the question: Is it possible they might be the Tesla of the air?

I believe that the key to the door is green hydrogen. This has close to zero carbon emissions as it is created by electrolysis powered by renewable energy such as solar and wind. There are several companies in the vanguard, notably ITM Power and Ceres. Moreover, green hydrogen can be stored, which would go a long way to solving the ongoing problem of renewable intermittency. I also cannot believe that the giants Shell and BP, as well as the big US companies, are sitting on the sidelines on a matter of such global importance. Indeed, maybe I am an optimist, but I suspect work is now going on amongst these major oil companies to develop sustainable fuels which will ultimately lead to a reduction in the use of petroleum jet fuels.

Finally, one might ask what the RAF is doing. Bearing in mind that the MOD is responsible for 50 per cent of central government greenhouse gas emissions, it is perhaps not so surprising that the RAF wants to achieve a really significant reduction using existing and emerging technologies. Well, I am delighted to report that its response is quite exciting. In November 2021, the RAF completed the world's first flight using a synthetic fuel and in doing so created a Guinness World Record. The plane was an Ikarus C42 microlight in a flight lasting ten minutes using Zero Petroleum's UL91 fuel.

Like many others, I am encouraged by what I have learned and totally reject the notion that flying could become the preserve of only the very wealthy. It is imperative for the whole global industry to make low carbon air travel as competitive as fossil fuels, and having reflected on what has been achieved in flying over the last one hundred years and more, I remain confident that the combination of technology and creative engineering will find the solution.

There are several other aspects in aviation development that may or may not impact on climate change, or even vice versa, which warrant attention. I find no sympathy at all with the UK Climate Change Committee (CCC) recommendation that there should be no net airport expansion. The committee also put forward the notion that there should be measures adopted to actively reduce the demand for flying. I find that quite extraordinary: just at a time when the UK is determined to play a bigger global role, which by definition means more aviation miles, this committee recommends the opposite. Of course, to reach the UK's net zero 2050 commitment it was not surprising that the UK government in September 2021 decided to substantially increase the so-called carbon value: the official benchmark which puts a price on the emissions associated with any airport expansion scheme. Nevertheless, one has only to look at the latest data from London Heathrow Airport which reports, 'It is absolutely possible to decouple passenger growth from a growth in emissions. Since 2005 while passenger numbers have grown by 25% there has been a 3% reduction in carbon remissions.' This is one of the many reasons that Heathrow must have its additional runway, despite the pathological dislike of the project by the current Prime Minister. Heathrow Airport has stated, on the record, that it is committed to achieving net zero, and I for one am confident it will do it. There are those who argue that Heathrow Airport is not suitable to be the hub for a global Britain but, again with my marketing hat on, I maintain that, like it or not, London is one the world's greatest cities and Heathrow is its entry point requiring decent access and facilities. As Juliet Samuel wrote in the *Daily Telegraph* on Saturday 29 February 2021, 'A "global" trade policy with no third runway is a joke.'

However, there is a newer element of air travel that does worry me and that is a growing fascination with space travel. There seem to be more and more flights into space by the ultra-wealthy who want to be 'space tourists'.

One could argue the same happened in the 1920s with playboy entrepreneurs who pioneered the development of aircraft design, but I do believe space tourism is different. Just when the global population has started to embrace the concept of climate change and is working so hard to reach net zero emissions, to have billionaires jetting into space on a joyride seems in poor taste. I can only ask the question: Should it be allowed or not? If it is, who is assessing its effect on planet Earth?

Additionally, it seems to me there is also a danger that these same billionaires and certain private companies will wrap round the world, itself a tiny planet, layers of fast-flying, low earth orbiting satellites. Were this to happen it will in effect mean a complete change to the dynamics of internet infrastructure. As J. Scott Christianson of the University of Missouri, Columbia wrote in the *Financial Times* on 9 December 2021:

> Planetary-Scale ISPs [Internet Service Providers] are something new with worldwide coverage whose services don't have to be defined by borders. Our leaders should seize this opportunity to set a new global standard for open, unfettered internet access that respects human rights and empowers individuals.

I believe he is right and politicians like myself who take a real interest have to challenge our leaders. However, it is also a wildly naïve view to imagine that an 'open, unfettered internet access', will respect 'human rights and empower individuals'. There will always be those who will want to take advantage, and this was perfectly illustrated in November 2021, when the Russians tested an anti-satellite weapon (ASAT). It caused shock waves around the world as no one had been forewarned, especially in the West. It was the fourth time that a satellite has been taken out by a missile and it sent a very clear message that Russia had the capability to shoot down satellites in low earth orbit up to 2,000 km from Earth. We should exercise caution before aspiring for global transparency, as not everyone shares the same lofty ideals. Thankfully, however, our own RAF has joined ranks with the new UK Space Command, set up in April 2021, as it has been recognised that access to space is now fundamental to military operations. Appendix IX shows what the new UK Space Command is aiming to do, and I am so pleased to quote that, 'UK Space command is located at RAF High Wycombe alongside RAF Air Command. This enables UK Space Command to build alongside UK's Space Operations Centre (UK Spoc) and anything else relevant in the future.'

We all know that in relation to space no nation can do it alone, so it is good news that the UK is part of the Combined Space Operations initiative which comprises seven nations: Australia, Canada, France, Germany, New Zealand, the United States and UK. Co-operation between countries is so often the key to success, as I found out when training as a pilot over sixty years ago with recruits from no less than seven other NATO countries: Turkey, France, Belgium, Holland, Denmark, Norway and Canada.

The other concern I have about the aviation industry is the increased reliance on technology and the subsequent reduction of emphasis on human input. I use the horrific example of the two Boeing 737 Max crashes where remote control took over the flying of the aircraft from the pilots. They could do nothing to override the controls as they hurtled to Earth, killing everyone on board, all 346 souls. The first crash took place on 29 October 2018 and the second, an Ethiopian Airways flight, less than six short months later on 10 March 2019. These are terrible tragedies. Every pilot is encouraged to trust his instruments, but until recently there was always an override manual mechanism to stop any fatal move. There is a massive 238-page report from the US Congress on these disasters and yet, almost on a daily basis, we still read of more and more developments to enable an aircraft to take off, fly and land automatically. I personally believe, and strongly, that there must be an override facility for every passenger-carrying aircraft.

I also believe the RAF needs to think very long and hard about the increasing role of computer simulations such as Gladiator, a £36m simulation system. It is forecast that about 30 per cent of flying training today can be synthetic but that this figure could rise, in the near future, to as much as 70 per cent. I appreciate the sense in having some simulated training, as it would allow war games to be recorded and analysed. However, I draw the line at any suggestion that the whole or even majority of the training can be done synthetically. I also express concern that there appears to be no thinking going on about a replacement for the Hawk T2, albeit its out of service date is 2040. This, I am afraid, has memories of the 1920s and 1930s when we were unprepared.

I suppose any review of aviation would be incomplete without a comment on the dreaded drones. I have taken an interest in and debated the control of drones both in and out of Parliament. They are now an established part of life the world over. They have a useful role in agriculture, surveying, photography and e-commerce, but unmanned aircraft can cause nuisance and present real safety risks, not least by unlicensed or inexperienced operators. There has been much talk about how to have some sort of automated equivalent of air traffic control for drones. There appears to be interesting work in progress at the University of Cambridge by Dr Bashar Ahmad, who claims to have devised a way to detect and prevent threatening drone activity by using statistical techniques and radar data to predict unusual flying patterns. Allied to this is the work of Prof. Simon Godsill, also at the University of Cambridge.

However, this is not a sector that is standing still, and we now see the Department of Transport proposing strict alcohol drink limits for operators in preparation for online aerial deliveries to be made by drone. The limits fall into three categories, but they are all considerably lower than for driving a car, but this reflects the potential to cause substantial harm to those on the ground or to other aircraft. These proposals come as part of the revamp of flight laws to encourage technologies such as aerial taxis. The CAA has given permission to Amazon to experiment with drones. However, the project has clearly hit difficulties as Amazon, despite achieving its first trial delivery on 7 December 2020, has now cut back its staff at Cambridge by one hundred. I love flying and am excited to think about the true potential of drones. However, I do think the French have a good point in banning them from all National Parks because they disturb the wildlife, not to mention the human enjoyment of nature.

Finally, I want to address the fascinating Hybrid Air Vehicles (HAV) Airlander Project which I think holds great hope for the future. I visited its offices in Bedford on 17 September 2021 with the objective to better understand the possibilities of the Airlander which last flew from Cardington on 13 June 2017, a flight of 3 hours 23 minutes. By chance, it was a glorious evening and I found myself sitting on my terrace, as I often do, at Caesar's Camp. As I looked down the long sweep of lawn, I moved my eyes up to the sky and there, silhouetted against the early evening sky, was Airlander, travelling at a leisurely pace from west to east. I watched it as it disappeared out of view towards Potton and Everton, only to return about twenty minutes later. I was utterly transfixed by it and only learned later that it was in fact its very last flight as it was released from its moorings, completely by accident, in early November.

I feel inspired by the Airlander, and it is certainly not a one-off. After all, it has developed from the Skyship 500, of which six were built in the period 1979–85, and followed by Skyship 600, of which ten were built. They fly all over the world at their own leisurely pace with almost no adverse carbon effect. This new Airlander, currently being worked on, will cost the best part of £300m for the entire project, which will include the building of the first three production ships. This is no fringe machine, at 97 m it is 5 m longer than its predecessor, the 600, and much more stable. It will be the biggest non-rigid airship and a sort of hybrid air vehicle. The only competition in the world comes from the German Zeppelin Company but its offering is much smaller. Airlander offers the ability to stay aloft for as long as three weeks at any one time with no crew or five days with a crew. What can it do? It is ideal for reconnaissance and as an early warning aircraft which is difficult to find because radar cannot pick it up; it can just sit passively. Additionally, it is so big it can provide a platform for a great many sensors. It does not even need a runway to take off and land, just an open field.

When I look at the UK's existing early warning aircraft, I am not filled with my usual optimism: we appear to have some old 707s, Sentinels which have been in service for between forty and fifty years. They are to be phased out and replaced by between six and eight Poseidon and three Boeing E-7a Wedgetails. The original plan had been for five Wedgetails but even three is a bit of a myth, as one will be used for training and another one will be in planned maintenance for at least some of the time. Whichever way you cut it, this is not a huge capability and I do believe it will leave us open to a huge credibility gap. A gap that could easily be filled by the military development of the Airlander.

The other market that is clearly opening up is what the *Financial Times* called 'the Flying Funship' in an article in October 2019 about the Airlander:

Inside the offices of Hybrid Air Vehicles is a simulator for a new type of luxury air travel that could buy the rich and adventurous birds eye

[sic] views of the Arctic and the Amazon without the need for runways.

Naturally, there are pessimists who point to the failure of the airships of the 1980s which could not find themselves a niche. But Airlander is not a small enterprise and its potential is huge: its fabric incorporates Mylar and Kevlar, and its cabin is built from fibreglass which makes it virtually invisible to radar. This is an anti-aircraft capability that is so different to anything else. It is not even part of the debate on sustainable fuel and yet this whole aircraft is sustainable itself. So, will it fly? Certainly the vision shown by the founders and the dedicated pioneering staff think they will make the breakthrough and I hope they will. As Richard Aboulafia, an aviation analyst at Teal Group points out:

> It's a technological road not taken. The odds that we would redo the evolutionary path are not all that great... You could do all these things (that Airlander 10 is designed for). Somebody just has to say, 'We're going down that path.'

My personal view with all the hindsight of eight-five years is it deserves to succeed; stranger technologies have been rubbished and yet have come good. So, yes, I believe it will fly again. This is a fitting point to bring this chapter to conclusion. We all know the challenges. The cynical will say zero carbon aviation technology is too slow to meet climate goals. However, they ignore the stark fact that the global usage of computers produces twice the amount of emissions of greenhouse gases as the aviation industry. I have always believed the moral in the fable of the Hare and the Tortoise: slow and thoughtful will win the race. In any case, so many of us are confident that green technology is the key to long term prosperity – for UK Aerospace, the global aviation industry and the planet as a whole – as such, the UK cannot fail, nor will it fail.

CHAPTER FIFTEEN
NATIONAL SERVICE REVISITED

The catalyst to write this book came from my own experiences of National Service from 1955 to 1957, allied to fact that no one had written in any depth about the experiences of RAF National Service pilots and specifically those who trained in Canada. This is quite incredible, really, when one considers that no less than 1.7 million young British men were called up to serve. The army led the way and took 1,244,416; the RAF 430,885 and the Royal Navy just 43,583. The last soldier was demobbed in May 1963.

There were many benefits to National Service, conceived and brought into being after the horrors of the Second World War. It ensured that the UK had trained forces at a time when voluntary recruitment would have fallen far short and thus exposed the UK's weakness on the global stage. Indeed, without National Service Britain could never have kept forces in the Middle East, Africa and Asia, nor could it have attempted to revitalise the Empire into a Commonwealth. There were also downsides; the principle one being that at its height in the 1950s there was a knock-on effect on British industry, which faced an acute shortage of manpower which affected all sizes of businesses. There were also some very real dangers, especially for those of us who served with the RAF. I highlight the number of RAF National Service pilots who gave their lives in their service to our country. The number killed in flying accidents was 3,145 and in service abroad, 484. Total 5,877. Some more statistics are included in the Appendix III.

I could have ended the book with the previous chapter, 'The Future of Aviation' but important as that is I wondered whether there was now a case to be made to look again, over half a century later, at the concept of service to one's country. For me, and many others, National Service offered a training of sorts for adulthood. Very few of the young men who were called up had ever left home or had to look after themselves before. Of course, they had all been to school but the scale and mix of backgrounds being thrown into it together created a bond and friendship that for many lasted a lifetime. No other generation has had this. Comradeship allied to discipline has, in my judgment, helped the UK succeed in facing the challenges of the modern world. Therefore, I would like to put forward the argument that National Service is a worthwhile endeavour and the concept of it worthy of discussion.

The broad concept that appeals to me would be one that would encompass all young men and women for just a year of their life at the age of eighteen. The proposition would be to do something worthwhile for society that would also be beneficial to the young person before they started life after school, whether that is university, college, an apprenticeship or work. I wonder if there should be any exemptions at all, except perhaps for those who provide medical or psychological grounds for doing so.

Life today, especially for our young people, is challenging. We are all faced with issues of diversity and equality which require tolerance and understanding. Britain is a wonderful melting pot of cultures with people of all different colour, creed and faith. National Service, properly executed, could be a celebration of this diversity by bringing young people together from all these different backgrounds to work on projects with a shared goal. They could work with the voluntary and charity sector (although I do think they should be paid the minimum wage), working with those on the fringes of society: the sick, elderly, vulnerable, etc. Or with the armed forces, the emergency services, the NHS. It would teach people to rub along together and appreciate each other. It might well include overseas travel to work on environmental or humanitarian projects, a modified and expanded version of Volunteer Services Overseas (VSO). In 2019/20 VSO enabled 4,158 volunteers to work in twenty different countries. The opportunities are endless.

There is the question of how to pay for it. I think those who are attached to the private sector should have their minimum wage paid by their employer, who should be able to set the cost against tax. The balance would be treated as a charitable payment. There may well be opportunities to attract resources from the philanthropic community, which is sizable in the UK.

It would have to be compulsory, but remember Attlee brought in the original National Service on a compulsory basis with support from all sides of the political spectrum.

Do I think the majority of young people would welcome it? Yes, I do. An independent report produced in May 2021 showed 130,000 youngsters were engaged in the Combined Cadet Force (CCF) across the country and the report celebrated the positive impact it had on these young people. In October 2021, the Duke of Edinburgh Award Scheme boasted 330,000 youngsters on its books; eighteen months after the pandemic took hold and put a stop to so many activities for our young people. To me, this bears testament to their desire to do some good for themselves and their country, and is far more beneficial than 'travelling during their gap year'.

I was intrigued to find out what the NATO countries with whom I flew in Canada are doing, and in summary: Turkey, Denmark and Norway still have a compulsory military service. Norway's includes women. Canada does not have a compulsory service and never did have one; Belgium suspended its programme in 1992 and France more recently in 2017, although it has introduced a new national civic service instead, for men and women. The Netherlands suspended its military service in 1997 but reintroduced a compulsory, modified military service on 1 January 2020, for both men and women. The net result is that of those countries which have had National Service in the past, only the UK and Belgium currently have nothing. In March 2018, a poll in the Brussels Times reported that two in three Belgians favour compulsory military or civilian service.

But I am not the first to raise the concept here in the UK and I pay tribute to those who have tried to float the idea, particularly my colleague Philip Hollobone MP who had an unsuccessful Private Members Bill in 2013: the details are in the Appendix VI. In May and June 2015, there were two quite long articles in the Telegraph concerning the topic: one focused on HRH Prince Harry's positive views of his service record and National Service, and the second, by Anita Singh, quoted a survey which found positive support across all age groups. So, for me, upon analysis, I find the case for one year of compulsory National Service by our talented young people to be even stronger than I had expected.

I would like to finish by returning to those of us who did serve as RAF National Service pilots, as we must all be over eighty years of age now and we are all, at times, in need of a little support. When family and friends are not available, this support comes from two very special organisations. The first I would like to mention was started in 2002, by a few former RAF National Servicemen. It is called the National Service (RAF) Association and its aims are to support its members by putting them in touch with each other and by organising regular social events. It appears to have met a need, as there are now no less than twenty-seven branches all over the UK and an excellent quarterly magazine, *The Astral*. The ethos of the wonderfully caring veterans who run this organisation is summed up in their definition of a veteran:

> A Veteran – whether active, retired, served one hitch, or on reserve – is someone who, at one point in their life, wrote a blank cheque made payable to 'My Queen and my country for an amount of up to and including my life'.

The second organisation is the more commonly known RAFA – Royal Air Force Association. For ninety years, it has been providing support to RAF personnel, active and retired, as well as their families. It is a truly remarkable organisation of which I have been a member for years and one I am proud to support. It is incredible to think they are in effect a good friend to more than 85,000 members of the RAF community and the range of services they offer is awe-inspiring: befriending and mental wellbeing services, training courses, professional childcare training for spouses, bespoke casework support and help to secure emergency grants. There is also the work of RAFA Kidz, which provides affordable nursery places for the children of RAF parents who may be frequently relocated.

For me, RAFA's response to the challenges of the Covid-19 pandemic has not only helped an enormous number of people, but has also shown that the association can move with the times while remaining committed to its original ideals and principles. In October 2021, I attended the annual dinner of the Lords & Commons Branch of the RAF Association at which Air Marshal Sir Baz North KCB OBE made an address. He spoke of the dramatic increase in demand for welfare support services that came with the onset of the pandemic and how, within days, the association was able to roll out a bespoke care package, supporting those in isolation, with the help of 800 new volunteers. In the following months, 35,000 potentially vulnerable people were contacted and supported, and from that emergency response was created RAFA's newest service, 'Connections for Life'. With Sir Baz's permission, I have printed in full the relevant parts of this outstanding speech in Appendix VII. He concluded with the RAFA's dedication:

In friendship and in service one to another, we are pledged to keep alive the memory of those of all nations who died in the Royal Air Force and in the Air Forces of the Commonwealth, in their name we give ourselves to this noble cause. Proudly and thankfully, we will remember them.

My experiences as a National Service pilot gave me so much and I remain ever grateful for them: the skills I learnt, the friendships I made and the values I have been proud to adopt as my own. Service has always played a very significant and worthwhile part of my life and I conclude with the words of Winston Churchill, quoted in the *New Yorker*, which I believe have resonance with us all: 'We make a living by what we get, but we make a life by what we give.'

Author takes to the air once again, aged eighty.

APPENDIX I

ORIGINAL NATIONAL SERVICE BILL

National Service Bill.

EXPLANATORY AND FINANCIAL MEMORANDUM.

1. The purpose of the Bill is to provide for compulsory service in the Armed Forces after 31st December 1948 when the present transitional arrangements described in the White Paper, Cmd. 6831, come to an end. The Bill will amend the National Service Acts, 1939 to 1946, in the following respects.

2. Liability is to be confined to male British subjects who have reached the age of eighteen years and have not reached the age of twenty-six years, and who have not served in the Armed Forces before 1st January 1947 (clauses 1 and 8). Provision is made for young men to be called up exceptionally at the age of seventeen years six months if they so desire (clause 14). Service other than service in the Armed Forces (apart from equivalent service by conscientious objectors) will no longer be required.

3. Under the present Acts persons called up are deemed to be entered or enlisted in the Armed Forces for the unspecified period of the emergency ; but those who joined the Forces before 1947 have been or will be released from service under the age and length of service scheme, whilst those called up during 1947 and 1948 will be released after serving for fixed periods ranging from two years to eighteen months (Cmd. 6831). The Bill provides that men called up after 1st January 1949 shall serve for eighteen months' whole-time service, or such shorter period as may be appointed by Order in Council, to be followed by five-and-a-half years' part-time service (clauses 1 and 2).

4. During their period of part-time service men may be required to undergo training not exceeding sixty days in all, of which they will not be compelled to serve more than twenty-one days in any year. A man may discharge his obligation for part-time service by serving as a volunteer in one of the auxiliary forces (clauses 2 and 3).

5. The Service Authorities will have the duty of providing, as far as practicable, further education within the meaning of section 41 of the Education Act, 1944, for men serving whole-time. Local education authorities, though absolved from the duty of providing further education for such men, will have power to assist in the provision of facilities for their further education by agreement with the Service Authorities (clause 10).

6. The reinstatement rights conferred by the Reinstatement in Civil Employment Act, 1944, will be preserved for men called up for whole-time service under the Bill, except that the minimum

[Bill 46]   A

House of Commons Parliamentary Papers Online.
Copyright (c) 2006 ProQuest Information and Learning Company. All rights reserved.

National Service Bill

229

ARRANGEMENT OF CLAUSES.

Clause.   *Service in the armed forces.*

1. Liability to be called up for service.
2. Whole-time and part-time service.
3. Volunteer service in lieu of part-time service.
4. Transfer.
5. Liability to complete interrupted service.
6. Calling up for training during part-time service.
7. Modifications of enactments relating to persons called up for service.
8. Transitional provisions.
9. Special provision as to medical and dental practitioners.

Education and Education Authorities.

10. Further education during whole-time service.
11. Information to be furnished by education authorities.

Reinstatement in civil employment.

12. Reinstatement in civil employment after whole-time service.
13. Rights of employees called up for training.

Miscellaneous amendments of the National Service Acts, 1939 to 1946.

14. Early registration and calling up.
15. Enforcement of requirement to submit to medical examination.
16. Other amendments.

Supplemental.

17. Postponement of liability to be called up for service.
18. Termination of reserve or auxiliary service by enlistment notice.
19. Laying of Orders in Council and regulations before Parliament.

House of Commons Parliamentary Papers Online.
Copyright (c) 2006 ProQuest Information and Learning Company. All rights reserved.

10 & 11 GEO. 6.   *National Service.*   **231**

A

B I L L

TO

Confine the operation of the National Service Acts to male British subjects and to service in the armed forces of the Crown; to make provision as to the terms and conditions of such service and as to the period for which those Acts shall continue in operation; and for purposes connected with the matters aforesaid.

A.D. 1947.

BE it enacted by the King's most Excellent Majesty, by and with the advice and consent of the Lords Spiritual and Temporal, and Commons, in this present Parliament assembled, and by the authority of the same, as follows :—

5   *Service in the armed forces.*

1.—(1) Subject to the provisions of the National Service Acts, 1939 to 1946, and this Act (which Acts are hereinafter collectively referred to as the National Service Acts), every male British subject who has attained the age of eighteen years and has not 10 attained the age of twenty-six years and is ordinarily resident in Great Britain shall, by virtue of this Act, be liable to be called upon to serve in the armed forces of the Crown for two terms of service that is to say—

Liability to be called up for service.

    (*a*) a term of whole-time service, that is to say, service in
15   the regular forces for a period of eighteen months or such shorter period as His Majesty may by Order in Council appoint; and

    (*b*) a term of part-time service as defined by this Act;

and save as aforesaid no person shall be liable to be called up for
20 service under the National Service Acts.

(2) The provisions of the National Service Acts, 1939 to 1946, as amended by this Act shall apply with respect to a person liable to be called up for service by virtue of this Act and to a person called up thereunder; and references in those Acts to a
25 person liable to be called up for service under the National

[Bill 46]   **A** 2

House of Commons Parliamentary Papers Online.
Copyright (c) 2006 ProQuest Information and Learning Company. All rights reserved.

iv   *National Service*   10 & 11 GEO. 6.

20. Expenses.
21. Interpretation.
22. Application to Scotland.
23. Application of National Service Acts to the Isle of Man.
24. Duration of National Service Acts.
25. Commencement, citation and repeal.

SCHEDULES.

First Schedule.—Length of whole-time service.

Second Schedule.—The Reinstatement Act.

Part I.—Modifications of the Act in relation to persons entering whole-time service after the commencement of this Act.

Part II.—Modifications of the Act in relation to persons entering whole-time service on or after the first day of January nineteen hundred and forty-seven taking effect on the passing of this Act.

Third Schedule.—Minor and consequential amendments of the National Service Acts, 1939 to 1946.

Fourth Schedule.—Local and Appellate Tribunals.

Fifth Schedule.—Enactments repealed.

House of Commons Parliamentary Papers Online.
Copyright (c) 2006 ProQuest Information and Learning Company. All rights reserved.

National Service (Amendment) Bill 521

EXPLANATORY AND FINANCIAL MEMORANDUM

1. This Bill proposes to increase the period of whole-time service of men called-up under the National Service Act, 1948, from 12 months to 18 months and to reduce their total period of whole-time and subsequent part-time service in an Auxiliary Force from 7 years to 5½ years. (Clauses 1 and 2).

2. It is proposed that registered medical practitioners and persons registered in the Dentists' Register under the Dentists' Acts, 1878–1923 should be liable to be called-up under the National Service Act up to the age of 30 instead of only up to the age of 26, which applies generally. (Clause 3).

3. The National Service Act, 1947 provided that no person who reached the age of 18 on or after 1st January, 1954 should be liable to be called-up unless a later date had been substituted by Order in Council approved by affirmative resolution of both Houses of Parliament. Under the National Service Act, 1948, which consolidates the earlier National Service Acts and the Reinstatement in Civil Employment Act, 1944, this Order in Council is not subject to approval by affirmative resolution of Parliament. The opportunity has been taken to correct this omission. (Clause 4).

4. Any charge on the Exchequer under this Bill will arise mainly in respect of the additional numbers with the Forces owing to the extension of the period of colour service of National Service men. It is not possible, however, to indicate whether any charge arising in this respect will exceed the cost of alternative measures which might, but for the proposals in this Bill, be necessary to sustain the Forces at the essential minimum strength to meet their defence commitments. (Clause 5).

[Bill 26]

House of Commons Parliamentary Papers Online.
Copyright (c) 2006 ProQuest Information and Learning Company. All rights reserved.

House of Commons Parliamentary Papers Online.
Copyright (c) 2006 ProQuest Information and Learning Company. All rights reserved.

National Service (Amendment) Bill 523

ARRANGEMENT OF CLAUSES

1. Substitution of eighteen months as term of whole-time service.
2. Substitution of five and a half years as aggregate of terms of whole-time and part-time service.
3. Limit of age for calling-up in case of medical and dental practitioners.
4. Draft of any Order under s. 61 of principal Act to be laid before Parliament.
5. Expenses.
6. Short title, construction and citation.

[Bill 26]

House of Commons Parliamentary Papers Online.
Copyright (c) 2006 ProQuest Information and Learning Company. All rights reserved.

NATIONAL SERVICE POSTINGS
TO THE ARMED FORCES

	Navy	Army	RAF	Total
1948	3,700	100,500	46,700	150,900
1949	8,100	115,400	43,100	166,600
1950	1,300	120,600	52,300	174,200
1951	2,728	18,376	47,547	168,651
1952	3,716	126,720	39,948	170,384
1953	3,544	113,611	36,909	154,064
1954	5,875	108,616	33,484	147,975
1955	6105	108,656	42,072	156,833
1956	4,350	89,479	36194	130,023
1957	2,727	77,832	29,586	101,165
1958	1,077	68,090	12,041	81,208
1959	255	49,739	11,234	61,228
1960	106	46,777	8,770	55,653
Total	43,583	1,244,416	430,885	1,718,884

Source: Official figures / Definitions Facts and Uncertainties from
Richard Vinen: National Service Conscription in Britain 1945–1963

DEATHS IN THE BRITISH ARMED FORCES
1 JANUARY 1948 – 31 DECEMBER 1960

Theatre of operation and service					
	Navy	Marines	Army	Air Force	Total deaths in theatre
Korea	46	28	1,031	30	1,135
Malaya	5	27	893	276	1,201
Palestine	0	2	176	17	195
Cyprus	4	13	274	67	358
Egypt/Suez	1	12	267	69	349
Kenya	0	0	69	25	94
Other (including UK)	2,457	154	8,185	5,393*	16,189
Total	**2,513**	**236**	**10,895**	**5,877**	**19,521**

* RAF deaths in UK primarily flying accidents in and after training

Source: Armed Forces Administration Agency, June 2005, best estimates

RAF STRENGTHS 1957–62

Date	National Service	Regular	Total	% of Regular
1.4.57 (actual)	68,700	153,900	222,600	30.86
1.4.58 (estimate)	46,700	141,300	188,000	24.84
1.4.59 (actual)	26,500	142,300	168,800	15.70
1.4.60 (estimate)	18,400	139,400	157,800	11.66
1.4.61 (actual)	13,400	131,800	145,200	9.23
1.4.62 (estimate)	5,400	128,900	134,300	4.02

This table demonstrates the decline in numbers of National Service

APPENDIX IV

SERVICE NUMBERS FOR RAF NATIONAL SERVICE

Service number batch	Dates of allocation	Quantity	Comment
2340000 / 2599999	1.47 – 7.53	260,000	non-ATC
2700000 / 2787999	7.53 – 2.56	88,000	non-ATC
3100000 / 3156537**	5.49 – c57	56,538	ex-ATC
5010251 / 5010916	2.56 – ?	666	non-ATC
5010917 / 5012250**	5.56 – ?	1,334	ex-CCF (RAF)
5012251 / 5012999	2.56 – 11.60	749	non-ATC postponement
5013000 / 5082226	2.56 – 11.60	69,227	non-ATC
5090000 / 5099999	5.57 – ?	10,000	granted postponement
5100000 / 5100357**	2.59 – ?	358	ex-CCF (RAF)
5190000 / 5194999	1.57 – ?	5,000	aircrew

** Signifies ex-ATC (Air Training Corp) or CCF (Combined Cadet Force RAF) recruit

Source: Both tables Memories of National Service John Hamlin/ Official

APPENDIX V

THE FIRST STAGES OF YOUR NATIONAL SERVICE IN THE RAF

THE FIRST STAGES OF YOUR NATIONAL SERVICE IN THE ROYAL AIR FORCE

Reporting Instructions

1. This leaflet will be of use to you now that you have been accepted for National Service in the Royal Air Force. In due course you will receive from the Ministry of Labour and National Service your Enlistment Notice and a railway warrant to Bedford.

2. If you have volunteered for aircrew duties then your Enlistment Notice will normally instruct you to report to R.A.F., Hornchurch, where you will remain for a few days before moving on to Cardington. Should the Enlistment Notice, despite your having volunteered for aircrew, require you to report to Cardington, then you must do so and inform the reception officer of your aircrew application.

Private Vehicles

3. If you own a private vehicle, which includes a bicycle, you must leave it at home as you are not allowed to have one during the first three months of National Service.

Personal Certificates

4. Be sure that you take with you, to Cardington, your National Insurance Card together with any educational or other certificates which will help to decide the trade for which you are most suitable.

Clothing

5. You will normally be at Cardington for seven days. Towards the end of that time your civilian clothes will be sent to your home. You should therefore take with you only essential clothing, including a change of underwear. You may take with you items of sports *clothing* if you wish.

6. If you are an aircrew volunteer and have been instructed to report initially to R.A.F., Hornchurch, then you will not be issued with any clothing until you subsequently report to Cardington. You should therefore take with you sufficient changes of shirts, socks and underwear for one week, bearing in mind that some of the tests at Hornchurch involve physical activity. Protective outer clothing will be issued to you for these tests.

7. So far, you have been told what you are to do and what you may not do. This may add to your natural reluctance to leave your home, your friends and all that is familiar for something which is to a large extent unknown. The object of this leaflet is to help you find your feet in your new surroundings. You will very quickly make new and staunch friends. There is much you can learn from them and something they can learn from you. There is no doubt that you will benefit from mixing with others and that you will finish your National Service a more mature, self-reliant and tolerant man. Your National Service can be a rewarding experience if you are determined to make it so. The R.A.F. will do its best ; the rest is up to you.

Arrival at Cardington

8. When you arrive at Bedford railway station you should report to the R.A.F. Regional Transport Officer (R.T.O.) whose office is on the platform. You will then be taken to R.A.F., Cardington, by transport.

9. Immediately you arrive at Cardington your particulars will be recorded, you will be shown your accommodation and then given a hot meal. You will be allotted to a Flight, in the charge of a Flight Commander, who is responsible for guiding you through the daily programmes and for your welfare.

Personal Matters

10. You cannot settle quickly into service life if you have some personal problem which is worrying you. Do not keep it to yourself. Ask your N.C.O. to arrange for you to see the Flight Commander. Problems are not always as difficult to settle as they seem and you will get all the help and advice possible.

Amenities

11. There are churches of three denominations at Cardington. In addition, there are church and N.A.A.F.I. clubs, television and a very good cinema. There is also a well equipped gymnasium and facilities for most sports.

Sports Kit

12. You will be issued with P.T. vests, shorts, plimsolls, football jerseys and stockings. Hockey sticks, football boots and other sports equipment are available on loan.

Letters Home

13. Your first evening at Cardington will, of course, be a busy one. It is all too easy to put off letter writing until later. Your people will be anxious to hear of your safe arrival, so write without delay. If you do not, you will not only cause your people unnecessary worry but you may add to the many enquiries the Station receives from worried relatives. (See special notice at end of leaflet.)

Medical Examinations

14. You will again be medically examined whilst at Cardington.

RAF MUSEUM
LIBRARY

Trades Information

15. You will be given the opportunity to see for yourself the trades which are available to National Servicemen and to learn something of the work those trades involve. You will later be interviewed by an experienced officer or N.C.O. who will help you to choose a number of trades for which you are eligible, and for which you wish to be considered.

16. Your wishes will be taken into account when provisionally selecting a suitable trade, but it is not always possible to place a National Serviceman in the trade of his choice.

17. If you claim to have civilian experience in a trade similar to an R.A.F. trade, then say so when you are interviewed. Show your interviewer any technical or educational certificates you possess. If it appears that you may be successful in a trade test, and that you are eligible, then you will be tested.

18. If you pass a trade test, and where necessary an education test, and there is a vacancy in the trade you will be given the rank, and the pay which goes with it, up to Junior Technician. The rank given will depend on how well you pass the trade test and you will only be given that rank and pay when you leave the School of Recruit Training. The pay will, however, be back dated from the day you were called up.

Uniforms and Kit

19. You will be given your kit and fitted with your uniforms. If you are outsize you will be measured for your uniforms and, if necessary, footwear will be made for you.

Pay

20. You will be given your first week's pay on the third or fourth day at Cardington.

21. Before you leave Cardington an accountant officer will explain to you all you need to know about your financial position as an airman. This will give you an opportunity to enquire about pay, allowances, National Service grants and so on. Do not hesitate to ask questions.

Schools of Recruit Training

22. At the end of your stay at Cardington, unless you are a volunteer for aircrew, you will go to one of the following Schools of Recruit Training: —

R.A.F., West Kirby	R.A.F., Bridgnorth
R.A.F., Padgate	R.A.F., Hednesford
R.A.F., Wilmslow	

The course at the school includes instruction in the following: —

History of the R.A.F.	General Education
R.A.F. Trades	Ground Combat Training
Drill and Physical Training	Reliability and Initiative Training

During the fifth week of training you will finally be allocated to a trade. The course ends with a passing-out parade followed by a week's leave before reporting to an R.A.F. station for a course of trade training, or for training " on the job ".

Aircrew and Pre-Selected Ground Branch Officers

23. If you are a volunteer for aircrew, and have been selected by the Aircrew Selection Centre at R.A.F., Hornchurch, you will go forward for aircrew training at the end of your stay at Cardington. Similarly, if you have been pre-selected for a commission in a ground branch, you will go to the Officer Cadet Training Unit, R.A.F., Jurby, direct from Cardington.

Education

24. During the first year of service National Servicemen are given two hours' compulsory education each week and one hour each week during the second year. Forces correspondence courses are available to all and a grant of £3. maximum. in any one year, is allowed to meet the cost of an airman's pursuit of further education.

Conclusion

25. This leaflet is intended to give you advance information which will help you in the initial stages of your National Service. It will apply to the majority but there may be changes in procedure to meet individual circumstances.

SPECIAL NOTICE TO MEN REPORTING FOR SERVICE IN THE ROYAL AIR FORCE

Private Mail

In order to ensure the expeditious delivery of your private mail it is in your own interest to advise all your correspondents to refrain from writing to you until you have received your service number and a definite service address. These particulars will be given immediately upon your arrival at the Recruit Centre and you should then inform your correspondents of your correct service address.

(5763) Wt. 44405—BN4083 30m 6/56 A.O.St

005068 006108

NATIONAL SERVICE BILL 2013

National Service Bill

A

BILL

To provide a system of national service for young persons; and for connected purposes.

Presented by Mr Philip Hollobone,
supported by Mr Stewart Jackson.

Ordered, by The House of Commons,
to be Printed, 24 June 2013.

© Parliamentary copyright House of Commons 2013
This publication may be reproduced under the terms of the Open Parliament Licence, which is published at
www.parliament.uk/site-information/copyright.

PUBLISHED BY AUTHORITY OF THE HOUSE OF COMMONS
LONDON — THE STATIONERY OFFICE LIMITED
Printed in the United Kingdom by
The Stationery Office Limited
£x.xx

Bill 32 (xxxxxx) 55/3

National Service Bill

CONTENTS

1 National service system
2 Scope of the scheme
3 Pay and tax allowance for participants
4 Interpretation
5 Financial provision
6 Offence
7 Regulations
8 Short title, commencement and extent

A

BILL

TO

Provide a system of national service for young persons; and for connected purposes.

BE IT ENACTED by the Queen's most Excellent Majesty, by and with the advice and consent of the Lords Spiritual and Temporal, and Commons, in this present Parliament assembled, and by the authority of the same, as follows: —

1   National service system

(1) Every individual who has attained the age of 18 years, and who has not attained the age of 26 years, shall be liable to serve one year of national service at some point between these years unless exempt.

(2) Exempt individuals are those with severe mental or physical disability.   5

(3) National service shall be defined as participation in a full time scheme accredited by HM Government as meeting the requirements of national service and set out in regulations by the Secretary of State.

(4) Non-exempt individuals who do not serve one year of national service before the age of 26 years shall be guilty of an offence.   10

2   Scope of the scheme

(1) Regulations shall provide that the scheme must extend the scope of the National Citizen Service and include the following elements —

    (a) educational assistance for those participants who have yet to attain basic educational requirements of reading and writing in English and   15
mathematics;

    (b) coaching and instruction to attain basic levels of physical fitness, personal discipline, smart appearance, self respect and respect for others;

    (c) instruction in personal financial budgeting, household bills, nutrition,   20
cooking, time keeping, life skills, tolerance towards others, treating elderly and disabled people with dignity and respect; and

    (d) instruction in basic aspects of the law in relation to the most common offences involving young people.

2

(2) Regulations shall also provide that the scheme shall include—

    (a) a residential element, requiring that participants live away from home; and

    (b) an element of public service, comprising one or more of the following to be chosen by the individual— 5

        (i) charitable work,

        (ii) social action,

        (iii) care for the elderly or disabled,

        (iv) overseas development activity, or

        (v) work connected with the National Health Service, the 10 emergency services or the Armed Forces.

3 Pay and tax allowance for participants

(1) Participants in national service shall be paid the national adult minimum wage during their year of service with accommodation and travel funded by the Secretary of State. 15

(2) Regulations shall provide that a person who has successfully completed their year of national service shall be presented with a national service certificate which shall entitle them to a lifetime income tax rate personal allowance 10 per cent above the personal allowance that would otherwise apply.

4 Interpretation 20

In this Act "national adult minimum wage" means the minimum wage as specified under section 2 of the National Minimum Wage Act 1998 and exemptions and modifications set out in section 3 of that Act shall not apply.

5 Financial provision

There shall be paid out of money provided by Parliament — 25

    (a) *any expenditure of the Secretary of State in consequence of this Act, and*

    (b) *any increase attributable to this Act in the sums which under any other Act are payable out of money so provided.*

6 Offence

Regulations shall provide for those guilty of an offence under section 1(4) to be 30 subject to a penalty.

7 Regulations

Regulations under this Act shall be made by statutory instrument and may not be made unless a draft of the regulations have been laid before, and approved by a resolution of, each House of Parliament. 35

8 Short title, commencement and extent

(1) This Act may be cited as the National Service Act 2013.

(2) This Act comes into force one year after Royal Assent.

(3) This Act extends to England and Wales.

SPEECH BY SIR BAZ NORTH, KCB CBE ADC
PRESIDENT OF THE RAF ASSOCIATION
at the Annual Dinner of the RAF Association
Lords and Commons Branch, 12 October 2021

MANY OF US last met in this room at the last Lords and Commons Branch dinner in March 2020, just days before our world was shaken by the impact of Covid-19. The pandemic has had a dramatic effect on all our lives and, as President of the RAF association, I have been acutely aware of the unprecedented impact that it has had on our RAF community.

The Association's unique position at the heart of our RAF community meant that within days of the pandemic breaking out, we began to see these effects at first-hand.

As much of our support was delivered face-to-face, we were immediately forced to revolutionise our services. Our respite care facilities could not remain open, face-to-face casework and befriending became impossible, and we were extremely concerned for the well-being of our most vulnerable sheltered housing residents across the UK.

At the same time, the demand for our welfare support services increased dramatically as the effects of isolation and social distancing became apparent.

We took immediate and decisive action, and I stand here today full of pride at the dramatic impact that our – your – charity has had on many thousands of people who found themselves in desperate need of support. Within days of the start of lockdown we mobilised our fantastic network of employees, volunteers and branches, together with over 800 new volunteers – from every walk of life – to help them. With their help we phoned 35,000 potentially vulnerable members of our RAF community to check on their welfare, and offer them practical, tangible support if they needed it.

Some were in dire need – running out of food and basic hygiene products. We mobilised nationwide and provided hundreds of emergency doorstep drops.

Many more people were experiencing acute loneliness and isolation, and, by the end of 2020, we had made over 109,000 friendship calls – supporting over 2,000 people on a weekly basis, generating over 16,000 new welfare cases.

From that emergency response we created our new Connections for Life service, and those vitally important calls – lifelines to so many – continue to this day. There are many of you in this room – individuals, companies, serving RAF personnel – who have first-hand knowledge of making those calls. I salute you all. You, very simply, have transformed people's lives.

We quickly established an on-demand helpline – and the experiences of those who called us for help were heartrending. Veterans whose spouse had died, distraught with guilt that their last memory of them was waving goodbye as an ambulance drove off. Fragile, vulnerable people experiencing domestic violence in the pressure cooker of lockdown; and so many, many more.

On a lighter but no less effective note, our rapidly established on-line entertainment service was viewed more than 1.5 million times across the world. It delivered a daily, wide-ranging schedule of interactive sessions – everything from low-impact fitness, tap dancing and drill tuition to concerts, sing-alongs and guest interviews. It kept spirits high in dark times and it brought our RAF community – serving and veteran – closer together.

In order to inform the development of these many welfare innovations, we embarked on a major research study, the first undertaken into the impacts of Covid-19 on the RAF community. Carried out to the highest academically recognised standards, it has provided vital evidence regarding the issues that our community faces now and in the future.

Some findings were worrying but not perhaps unsurprising: high levels of loneliness, pressure on carers and many people facing ongoing underlying physical and mental ill health.

Others were reassuring: in the best tradition of the Royal Air Force, those surveyed were more concerned for the physical and mental welfare of their friends and family than for themselves. I'm sure that you will agree that this says a lot about our RAF community.

The research findings backed up the importance of supporting the resilience of individuals within our community and relieving key elements of everyday life which can cause pressure.

We quickly adapted our 'Finding it Tough' mental well-being programme, first launched in this very room only days before the pandemic hit. The FiT training helps people to recognise that everyone struggles with life from time to time. It is the first of its kind, as we have designed the content specifically for non-serving members of the RAF Whole Force who want to improve their own mental well-being or to support friends, community members and colleagues. I know that there are several defence industry partners here whose employees have benefited from the training and I thank those here whose support has made the continuation of this programme possible.

Based on other research we had undertaken, we launched an initiative designed to help 9 per cent of serving RAF personnel who have unpaid caring responsibilities for an older adult and have since widened this out to the wider RAF community. Known as 'Navigating Dementia', the service complements the support already provided by the RAF by creating a peer support network and a vital knowledge hub.

On RAF bases, our three RAFA Kidz nurseries, over eighty contact houses and free Wi-Fi, used over 150,000 times in 2020, all made significant contributions to the resilience of our serving personnel and their families.

But make no mistake – behind the scenes it has been tough. We have been working hard to ensure the future of the RAF Association. As with all charities, the Association's ability to fundraise has been severely affected. To protect our financial standing we furloughed as many employees as was practical – over 50 per cent. It was tough on them, and tough on the small cohort left, whose efforts were frankly herculean. We rapidly took measures to generate savings of c. £2 million, and the reserves we had built up, precisely for such an eventuality as the pandemic, have been heavily drawn upon to sustain our increased welfare outputs. In fact, in 2020, we spent more on welfare than in any previous year – £15 million. That was £2 million more than in 2019, and almost triple that spent in 2013. We continue to make wise and efficient use of our reserves: 87p of every pound that the Association raised is spent on welfare outputs.

Your Association has played a central coalescing role in the RAF community for over ninety years and the values of kindness, friendship and mutual support that this charity embodies are as important today as they ever have been.

So, to the future. Our community numbers some one million people and the Association's role is to provide practical, life-changing support for all who need it. We are here to build futures, and we have ambitious plans for 2022 and beyond. In particular we plan to further expand our connections for life service, support for mental and physical well-being, our support for carers and our provision of sheltered housing.

My Lords, Ladies and Gentlemen: our RAF community is strong, and it is worth our support. Together we can resolutely face the challenges of the future. I ask you to stand and join me in the Association's dedication.

In friendship and in service one to another, we are pledged to keep alive the memory of those of all nations who died in the Royal Air Force and in the Air Forces of the Commonwealth. In their name we give ourselves to this noble cause. Proudly and thankfully we will remember them.

MINUTE SILENCE

APPENDIX VIII

THE FIRST AIRCRAFT FLYING CASUALTY

THOMAS ETHOLEN SELFRIDGE (8 February 1882 – 17 September 1908) has the unfortunate honour of being the first person to perish in a motorised aircraft accident, a passenger on a demonstration flight in the Wright Military Flyer piloted by Orville Wright. He was a First Lieutenant with an aviation background – amongst other achievements, in early 1908 he had been assigned to the Alexander Graham Bell-funded Aerial Experiment Association, where he had designed the Red Wing, the Association's first powered aircraft. Selfridge was also the first active duty member of the US military to die in a crash while on service.

On 17 September 1908, Wright demonstrated his Flyer at Fort Myer, Arlington County, Virginia, to the US Army Signal Corps division, as the army was contemplating a contract to buy aircraft from the Wright brothers. With the combined weight of the two men at 320 lbs, the plane had a heavier load than it had ever had before and, according to eye-witnesses, take-off was consequently a slower process.

At a height of 150 ft, the Flyer successfully circled Fort Myer a few times before a propeller broke, resulting in a loss of thrust. The aircraft began to shake violently and the splintered propeller hit a guy wire which was bracing the rear vertical rudder. The wire was whipped out of its fastening and demolished the already stricken propeller. The rudder spun to horizontal, sending the plane into a nose dive.

Wright shut off the engine and attempted to steady the Flyer to glide to safety, but the plane continued its nose dive. Pilot and passenger were thrown forwards against what was left of the wires, with Selfridge hitting one of the wooden uprights of the framework. On impact, Selfridge was found beneath the engine, under the wreckage, with a fracture to the base of his skull. Despite undergoing neurosurgery, he died three hours later without ever regaining consciousness. Wright was hospitalised for seven weeks with critical injuries, including a broken femur and ribs.

In a letter to his brother Wilbur, Orville described the catastrophic accident:

On the fourth round, everything seemingly working much better and smoother than any former flight, I started on a larger circuit with less abrupt turns. It was on the very first slow turn that the trouble began. ... A hurried glance behind revealed nothing wrong, but I decided to shut off the power and descend as soon as the machine could be faced in a direction where a landing could be made. This decision was hardly reached, in fact, I suppose it was not over two or three seconds from the time the first taps were heard, until two big thumps, which gave the machine a terrible shaking, showed that something had broken. ... The machine suddenly turned to the right and I immediately shut off the power. Quick as a flash, the machine turned down in front and started straight for the ground. Our course for 50 feet was within a very few degrees of the perpendicular. Lt. Selfridge up to this time had not uttered a word, though he took a hasty glance behind when the propeller broke and turned once or twice to look into my face, evidently to see what I thought of the situation. But when the machine turned head first for the ground, he exclaimed 'Oh! Oh!' in an almost inaudible voice.

Photographs taken of the Flyer, before Wright and Selfridge took to the air, show that Selfridge was bare-headed, while Wright was only wearing a cap. As speculation grew that Selfridge may have survived the crash if he had been wearing appropriate protection, it became compulsory for first pilots of the US army to wear large, heavy headgear, similar in style to early American football helmets.

Thomas Selfridge was buried with full military honours in Arlington Cemetery, neighbouring Fort Myer, and the cemetery's Selfridge Gate is named after him. The Selfridge Air National Guard Base, in Michigan, is also named in his honour. He was inducted into the National Aviation Hall of Fame in 1965.

Source: James Selfridge, Sandy, Bedfordshire, November 2021

UK SPACE COMMAND

Space, and our assured access to it, is fundamental to military operations. Loss of, or disruption to, the space domain, will impact our ability to undertake the majority of Defence Tasks, and has the potential for significant effect on civilian, commercial and economic activity. The threat from adversaries in this rapidly evolving operational domain is real and it is here now. If we fail to understand how to operate in space, integrate space with all domains and integrate with Allies and Partners space capabilities, we lose our competitive edge. This year's establishment of a space command for Defence was a crucial step in the development of a coherent strategy to understand and operate in space to protect UK interests.

Following its formation on 1 April 2021, UK Space Command formally stood up on 29 July 2021. As a Joint Command, it is staffed by personnel from the Royal Navy, British Army, and Royal Air Force, as well exchange officers from other nations, civil servants, and commercial partners. It brings together three functions under a single 2-Star military commander, Air Vice-Marshal Paul Godfrey: Space operations; space workforce training and growth; and space capability (developing and delivering space equipment programmes).

UK Space Command works alongside the Ministry of Defence Space Directorate, which is responsible for policy, strategy and cross-Government and international coordination. Direction from the National Space Council flows through the MOD Space Directorate to UK Space Command and other relevant elements of Defence. UK Space Command interacts with the UK Space Agency, when required, to deliver joint national space capability. UK Space Command has extremely close links to UK Strategic Command and Dstl, specifically in capability growth, enabling multi domain integration and capitalising on the rich pedigree of research and development expertise that exists within UK Defence.

UK Space Command is currently located at RAF High Wycombe, alongside RAF Air Command. This is allowing UK Space Command to build on existing RAF Space structures, such as the UK's Space Operations Centre (UK SpOC).

UK Space Command is being delivered by a change programme that is progressing on a conditions-based timeline. The roadmap sets out the transfer of operational capabilities and authorities, and the growth in capability and workforce, in conjunction with Defence, civil, and commercial stakeholders to develop and deliver the required space capability for defence.

Collaboration with international partners is key in space, no nation can do it alone. UK Space Command is continuing the UK's commitment to the Combined Space Operations initiative, which comprises seven nations (Australia, Canada, France, Germany, New Zealand, UK and US). This initiative seeks to improve cooperation, coordination, and interoperability opportunities in space. Its main effort is to ensure a safe, secure and stable space domain'. UK Space Command will also take command of the UK's participation in the US-led Space Coalition under Operation OLYMPIC DEFENDER and support the growth of the NATO space enterprise.

At Full Operating Capability, UK Space Command will provide command and control of all of Defence's space capabilities, including the UK SpOC, RAF Fylingdales, SKYNET and other enabling capabilities. It will have oversight of all space-based capability development, ensuring that space-based capabilities are developed in a way that ensures they can be integrated coherently with other Defence capabilities (and other domains). This includes joint enabling capability sponsored and delivered by UK Strategic Command along with the Dstl Space S&T programme. It will also have responsibility for the recruitment, training and development of Defence personnel working in the space domain.

BIBLIOGRAPHY

1936 John F. Leeming, *Airdays*, London: Harrap

1944 John Pudney and Henry Treece, *Air Force Poetry*, London: John Lane; The Bodley Head

1945 Eric Partridge, *A Dictionary of RAF Slang*, Michael Joseph Ltd

1972 B.S. Johnson, *All Bull: The National Servicemen*, Crescent

1978 Hugh Verity, *We Landed by Moonlight: Secret RAF Landings in France 1940–1944*, Ian Allan Ltd

1984 J. Rawlings, *The History of Royal Air Force*, Quartet

1986 Trevor Royle, *The Best Years of Their Lives: The National Service Experience 1945–63*, Michael Joseph

1993 L.V. Scott, *Conscription and the Attlee Governments: The Politics and Policy of National Service 1945–1951*, Oxford: Clarendon Press

1999 M. Sharpe, *History of Royal Air Force*, Paragon Plus

2000 Antoine de Saint-Exupéry, *Wind, Sand and Stars*, London: Penguin Books

2004 Tom Hickman, *The Call-Up: A History of National Service*, London: Headline Publishing

2013 Ian Watson, *Fading Eagle: Politics and Decline of Britain's Post-War Air Force*, Fonthill

Bernard O'Connor, *Churchill's Most Secret Airfield: RAF Tempsford*, Amberly

2014 Richard Vinen, *National Service: Conscription in Britain, 1945–1963*, Allen Lane

2018 James Holland, *RAF 100: 1918–2018: The Official Story*, London: Andre Deutsch

I wish to thank the House of Lords Library for obtaining all these books for my research.

ACKNOWLEDGEMENTS

I MUST START by thanking my three National Service RAF friends all alive and well today, Tony Collins, John Robbins and Brian Stevens, who were with me all the way through our training to become RAF pilots. I have consulted them about this book and their contributions have been outstanding and invaluable. The other friend from my RAF days is Lord David Cobbold, and his wife, Chryssie, who assembled no end of information, particularly about our fifty-year reunion, as well as the introduction to Tony Haigh Thomas, without which Chapter Thirteen would be all the poorer.

My initial research included visits to the Shuttleworth Trust at Biggleswade, of which I am a Life Member. My particular thanks go to the Chief Executive, Rebecca Dalley, and two volunteers, Jim Greaves and Jim Box, who solved the mystery of the wartime record of my boss in Colombo. Equally close to home is the former RAF Tempsford, with its Gibraltar Barn now owned and cared for by my good friend Merlin, Earl Erroll. He laid on and shared a very special visit with me, for which I am very grateful.

No book on the RAF would be possible without the help of the following: The RAF Museum which I visited twice and say a huge 'thank you' to Maggie Appleton, MBE and her team who went to considerable lengths to respond to my enquiries. The Air Historical Branch, RAF Northolt – there can be few men who know more about the RAF than Sebastian Cox as head of this branch, a big 'thank you' to Seb and to Lee. The Royal Air Force Association (RAFA) – an organisation so special to all who serve in the RAF, with my particular thanks to Cate Driscoll.

Canada remains a very special place to me, and I am grateful to many people connected to the country for their help with this book: William 'Bill' March, one of the RCAF's official historians, as well as my brother Crispin and his partner, Kathy, on Vancouver Island, for their help 'on the ground'. In addition, there was support from the Canadian High Commission in London, with particular thanks to Joanne Sommerville.

RAF Cardington features heavily in the book, so it was a privilege to be briefed by Andrew Barber, Head of Airworthiness for Hybrid Air Vehicles on the Airlander, and I am grateful to him for his time and for sharing some of his expert knowledge with me. RAF Cardington also features in the material on former Old Boys of Bedford School, including myself, who were RAF Pilots, all put together by the Director of the Bedford School Association, Hugh Maltby. Thank you, Hugh.

I would also like to mention the Air Industry in the UK, where so much is going on and so many have helped. I must also include ACOG (Aerospace Change Organising Group) with its plan to modernise Aerospace, ATI (Aerospace Technology Institute), which leads on the advance of green aircraft technology, and especially Rolls-Royce with its net zero mission. Its work is inspirational and gives me great optimism for the future of aviation.

The House of Lords Library staff has been superb in tracking down historical material and reminding me of the procedures of Parliament. The source books are listed in Appendix X.

To my youngest son, Jocelyn, for picking up the mantle of my limited collection of Biggles books to become a library in itself, now with fifty titles, and to my granddaughter Ciara for helping with the photography. To the production team at Unicorn, but especially to my editor, Lucie Skilton.

Finally, to my dear wife, Ann, for her encouragement, always, and particularly for the loan of the dining table for two years.